YOUR recipe could appear in our next cookbook!

T0028177

Share your tried & true family favorites with us instantly at

www.gooseberrypatch.com

If you'd rather jot 'em down by hand, just mail this form to...

Gooseberry Patch • Cookbooks – Call for Recipes
PO Box 812 • Columbus, OH 43216-0812

If your recipe is selected for a book, you'll receive a FREE copy!

Please share only your original recipes or those that you have made your own over the years.

Recipe Name:

Number of Servings:

Any fond memories about this recipe? Special touches you like to add
or handy shortcuts?

Ingredients (include specific measurements):

Instructions (continue on back if needed):

Special Code: **cookbookspage**

Over ➴

Extra space for recipe if needed:

Tell us about yourself...

Your complete contact information is needed so that we can send you your FREE cookbook, if your recipe is published. Phone numbers and email addresses are kept private and will only be used if we have questions about your recipe.

Name:

Address:

City: State: Zip:

Email:

Daytime Phone:

Thank you! Vickie & Jo Ann

Gooseberry Patch

Christmas
for Sharing

Delicious recipe favorites for making memories
with those you love.

Gooseberry Patch

An imprint of Globe Pequot
64 South Main Street
Essex, CT 06426

www.gooseberrypatch.com
1•800•854•6673

Do you have a tried & true recipe...

tip, craft or memory that you'd like to see featured in
a **Gooseberry Patch** cookbook? Visit our website at
www.gooseberrypatch.com and follow the
easy steps to submit your favorite family recipe.
Or send them to us at:

Gooseberry Patch
PO Box 812
Columbus, OH 43216-0812

Don't forget to include the number of servings your recipe makes,
plus your name, address, phone number and email address. If we
select your recipe, your name will appear right along with it...
and you'll receive a **FREE** copy of the book!

Contents

Dedication

Christmas is for sharing...yummy cookie recipes, gift-giving secrets, tree-trimming time, favorite sledding hills, frosty caroling walks and precious time with your family & friends.

Appreciation

Heartfelt thanks to all of you who shared your most treasured, tried & true recipes for the festive season.

Memories
for Sharing

Christmas
for Sharing

Magical December Memories

Carolyn Tellers
Erie, PA

When I was growing up, December was a magical time, from the first snowflake falling, to Christmas and New Year's. When I was 2-1/2 years old, my little brother was born, the week before Christmas, followed by my little sister, a few years later in February. We enjoyed "helping" Mom and Dad make cookies, especially putting the sprinkles on. We watched classic specials like "*A Charlie Brown Christmas*," "*Rudolph, the Red-Nosed Reindeer*" and "*Frosty the Snowman*." Every Sunday evening in December, we went to my paternal grandparents' house for dinner with relatives. Afterwards, Papa played the piano and we all gathered around to sing carols.

On Christmas Eve, my maternal grandparents came over, and we had delicious cocktail shrimp and dip for appetizers. For dinner, we had Mom's lentil soup and fried shrimp, Slovak Bobalky (sweet bread balls), rice and veggies. Sometimes we had ice cream treats in fun Christmas shapes for dessert, alongside homemade cookies. After dinner, one of my parents or grandparents would take my siblings and me into one of the bedrooms and read us a story. A short while later, we would hear a hearty "Ho, ho, ho! Merry Christmas!" We raced down the hallway to the living room to find the room dimly lit except for the lights from the Christmas tree, with beautifully wrapped presents underneath. Afterwards, my grandparents took us to their house in the country, and we sang Christmas carols along the way.

On Christmas morning, Grandma fixed a big brunch with baked ham, scalloped potatoes, veggies and treats. If there was snow on the ground, we had fun sledding down their hill. For Christmas dinner, we went to my other grandparents' house for roast turkey and all of the delicious fixings. After dinner, there were presents and a sing-along. I loved the times when my relatives from out of town were able to be with us! I treasure all these memories, especially the time spent with my beloved grandparents and other relatives who are no longer with us.

Memories
for Sharing

Christmas Progressive Dinner

Sandra Turner
Fayetteville, NC

One of my favorite Christmas memories was the progressive Christmas dinner my husband and I used to have with three other couples. We'd start at the first home for light appetizers, the second home provided soup and salad, the third home was the main meal and we all finished at the last home with desserts. Since we all live in different parts of the county, we planned the meal to start at one side of town and the last stop at the far end, so we didn't spend too much time driving from each location. The drive was enjoyable as we were able to see Christmas decorations all around town and in neighborhoods that we wouldn't usually travel through. It was a joy to see how our friends had decorated their homes for the holidays. The food and fellowship were enjoyable, too. To help with timing, the couple serving the next part of the meal would leave ten minutes ahead of the other couples, so that they could have everything ready at their home when the other couples arrived. After dessert, we had a low-cost gift exchange. We enjoyed this progressive Christmas dinner so much that we had it for 3 years. Unfortunately, due to health and mobility issues, we weren't able to continue this tradition, but the memories we made together will live on forever. I would be delighted to know that my story has encouraged others to plan their own Christmas progressive dinners, too.

I wish we could put up some of the Christmas spirit
in jars and open a jar of it every month.

–Harlan Miller

Christmas
for Sharing

Live Christmas Nativity

*Sheila Galus
Mantua, OH*

I was born in Niagara Falls, New York. We moved to Ohio in 1972 when I was seven. Every year we would go back home to spend the holidays with our family. My grandparents were the best...they knew how to make the holidays special! Every year, their church put on a "live nativity." My grandparents volunteered every night, helping with the costumes and serving hot coffee, cocoa and doughnuts to those who came to see it. Organ music would be playing in the background, and it was absolutely magical. Some of the men from the church, including my grandfather and Pastor Devine, built the whole manger from scratch. It was so beautiful to see the real meaning of Christmas reenacted. One time, one of the animals, I think it was the cow, got loose and my gramp, the pastor and a few of the other men had to chase it back to the church. It was walking right down the middle of the road! There was even a picture of it in the paper. Those were the best times growing up...those memories I hold dear.

Christmas...that magic blanket that
wraps itself about us.

–Augusta E. Rundel

Memories
for Sharing

Christmas Lights

Donna Landwehr
Wheat Ridge, CO

One of my favorite and funniest Christmas memories is of my mom putting up the Christmas tree. She worked during the week and always had a million things to do over the weekend, so she usually put up the tree later in the evening on Sunday. Mom would pull out all the decorations and get set to putting on the lights, only to find out the lights didn't work...again! She'd fight and fidget with the lights for about half an hour. Then she'd give up and run to the nearest store to get new lights, around 8:30 on that Sunday night, and spend until 10 or so finishing the tree. Every year, she'd fight the lights, then go to the store at 8:30. It's a special memory we always teased her about.

Silver Tinsel Tree

Jane Hrabak
Belle Plaine, IA

One of my most favorite memories of Christmas as a child has to be the little silver tinsel tree my parents put in the living room window for all to see. Looking back, I guess we didn't have much money. Aside from a handful of silver balls, most of the ornaments were made of heavy aluminum foil, including the star on top that Mom had made of foil. But what was most amazing to me was the colored light disk that revolved under the tree, glowing up through the branches and making beautiful light changes as it slowly turned around. I could watch it for hours! I remember running outside in the cold to watch the colored lights, and to let my parents know how perfect the tree looked, perched on our coffee table in the window for all to see.

Christmas
for Sharing

Little Christmas Angel

Katie Wollgast
Troy, MO

When I was a little girl, we attended a beautiful old Lutheran church. Its sanctuary had a towering ceiling. Tall stained-glass windows lined each wall beside the wooden pews. At Christmas, a huge tree was placed in the front and decorated to perfection. Because I was so little, I had no real part in the Christmas programs other than to be in the front with the other children. I don't remember anything from the programs themselves, other than all the adult faces staring back at us as we children crowded around the lower branches of the tree. I do remember going to the church basement before and after the program with the kind ladies who were our teachers. After one program, they pulled handmade angel ornaments from a big basket and gave one to each of us. The angels were made from Christmas fabric and lace, with little wooden balls for their heads. Their tiny faces were painted on and each had a little golden garland halo. Unlike some homemade ornaments, these were really beautiful. I loved mine from the beginning and kept it safely in my tiny hand. That little angel has hung on the family tree and now my own tree every Christmas since then. And every time I hang it up, I see myself as a little girl in the church basement, holding out my hand for my little Christmas angel. I think of those sweet ladies, many who are now gone, who gave me such a special memory.

It is Christmas in the heart
that puts Christmas in the air.

–W. T. Ellis

Memories
for Sharing

Christmas Toy Memories

Sandy Coffey
Cincinnati, OH

Our family didn't have much money in the early 1950s, but oh, how I loved circling my favorites in the toy catalog. Blue for all the items I would love and red for the really important things. Our stockings were a big nylon hosiery filled with small toys, candy and oranges. I loved the years when I got a walking doll, shoe skates, a dollhouse, a red swing and books. My family loves hearing this story every Christmas Eve, as it is tales from "Gram the Great"...that's me! To this day, I still have all those favorite toys except the well-used dollhouse. I love sharing them with the grandchildren and now the great-grandchild. It makes them appreciate the little things they get and not so much the big expensive items. Never a dull Christmas back then and now... memories in the making!

Best Little Christmas Tree Ever

Linda Graff
Powell, WY

Three years into our marriage, my husband decided to go back to school full-time. We moved to Butte, Montana, where he attended school and I worked. We did not have much money. Our final Christmas in Butte, my husband and a friend went into the mountains to get a Christmas tree for us. They found a beautiful one and cut it down. But when it hit the ground, the top came off! While the friend was quite upset, my husband decided to bring it home to me anyway. I loved it! I think it was only 18 inches tall. The house we rented was quite small and it was the perfect size for the space we had. Now we have been married more than 40 years, and we still have fond memories of that little tree.

Christmas
for Sharing

Christmas Ornament Party

Nan Scarborough
Farmerville, LA

One Christmas season several years ago, I sat down, tired and exhausted. I thought, the holidays are not supposed to be this way! So I decided to start a family tradition for the moms who are so furiously running around trying to make a perfect Christmas. I invited all the women in my family to my home for an evening of relaxation, creativity and just bonding. It was for the women only, the kiddos stayed home with Dad. I had snacks and Christmas music ready, and had chosen an easy handmade ornament for each of us to make. The first year was a felt gingerbread man. I had the cut-outs ready, needles and thread and all kinds of trims to choose from. It was such a great evening of fun, laughter and relaxation. This became a yearly tradition. It was a time when each of us looked forward to one night of no stress, no shopping, no cooking. Since then, I have moved far away from them, but my friends have carried on the tradition, and all the young girls who are now grown with family of their own have started the same tradition too.

At Christmas, when old friends are meeting
We give that long-loved joyous greeting...
"Merry Christmas!"
–Dorothy Brown Thompson

Memories
for Sharing

Christmas Blessing Basket

Marcia Jackson
Bolingbrook, IL

Our granddaughter Gracie came to live with us in 2004, when she was 2-1/2 years old. Because we live a thousand miles from the rest of our family, I wanted to start a few traditions with her. We place all of our Christmas cards in our "Blessing Basket" when we receive them, then we take one card out each day. It gives us a chance to talk about these people, many of whom we do not see very often, how they have touched our lives in special ways. Then at our family prayer, we ask a special blessing for the person or family whose card we selected. Gracie turns 21 in 2023, and the blessing basket is the first thing Gracie asks us to bring out every year. Traditions start young!

Christmas Ornaments Make Memories

Rebecca Meadows
Hinton, WV

At our house, Christmas tree decorating is the most fun and memorable activity. I have a tradition that each place I visit, I buy an ornament. The ornament may have the name of the place I visited or something that commemorates the trip. Then as we decorate the Christmas tree together, we recall all our fun memories. It's even more special when we have visitors who ask about certain ornaments. We get to tell stories about why we chose each ornament, stories of the places we went and events that happened. Some bring heartfelt memories and some bring such laughter, but the Christmas ornament memories are shared for years to come.

Christmas
for Sharing

Candy for Christmas

Pam Hooley
LaGrange, IN

When I was young, we were not a wealthy family, in the way of money, that is. So we four children rarely enjoyed candy. It was not in the budget, and as our mom said, it was bad for our teeth. But at Christmas time, we had the special treat of homemade candy. Mom would get together with her sister-in-law and the two of them would make candy all day...what delights! I even remember them making vinegar candy one year. Also, when my mother's extended family would get together for Christmas celebration, Grandma would fill a huge bowl with real candy from the store! She would go around to each one of us, not setting the bowl down until she was sure that all had taken a handful of sweet deliciousness! The bowl was then placed on the table for all to partake throughout the day...that was so special. What wonderful memories!

Christmas is the family time,
the good time of the year.

–Samuel Johnson

Memories
for Sharing

The Sweetest Bells
I Never Heard

Arlene Coury
San Antonio, TX

My grandmother used to hang colored foil-wrapped milk chocolate bell ornaments on her Christmas tree every year. There was one for each grandchild, to be eaten and enjoyed on Christmas Day. I can remember as a very small child gazing up at those hollow chocolate bells, wrapped in thin, delicately colored foil, hanging so gracefully by a thin gold thread. I could hardly wait for Christmas Day to arrive, so that my sister, brother, cousins and I could enjoy the melt-in-your-mouth goodness of that milk chocolate ornament. My grandmother hung these edible chocolate bells for us to enjoy, each and every year! It seems that the smallest traditions are the most treasured. She has been gone for many years now, but I have carried on this tradition for my own family, although I can no longer find the chocolate bells of years past. Chocolate, foil-wrapped ball ornaments now adorn our Christmas tree, tempting my children and grandchild. Sweet memories!

It is good to be children sometimes,
and never better than at Christmas.

–Charles Dickens

Christmas
for Sharing

There Really is a Santa Claus

Lorraine Pollachek
Boca Raton, FL

Very possibly the first Christmas of my life that I recall specifically was when I was around seven years old, which would have been 1965. On Christmas Eve, my mother took my two sisters and me to visit some nearby friends for the evening. We played for awhile, then we all fell asleep watching television. After awhile, Mom woke us and took us home. We lived in an up-and-down duplex with a long layout. When you came in through the kitchen door, you could see all the way down the single hallway to the living room picture window. When we got home, the only lights on in the house were the lights on the Christmas tree. All of our presents were laid out in a big semicircle around the tree in front of the picture window. I no longer remember all the gifts we received, but I remember clearly the best of those gifts, and I remember my older sister saying, "There really is a Santa Claus!" The very best of all was that I got the thing I wanted most, a "Budding Beauty" vanity, which was a plastic version of a lady's dressing vanity. To top it off, whether by fate or design, my aunt gave me a Barbie-style fashion doll with her own vanity and little bottles and jars that really opened. As it turned out, while we slept, my mom, her friend's teenage son and a couple of his friends, who I now realize were surely Santa's helpers, had hurried to our house to help Mom lay out the gifts quickly and get back before we woke.

It is good to be children sometimes,
and never better than at Christmas.

–Charles Dickens

Memories
for Sharing

Christmas in the Late 60s

Ann Turner
Garner, NC

I remember Christmas as such an exciting time. Although I knew it was Jesus's birthday, there was a lot of emphasis on Santa Claus too. My mother would always sing *"Santa Claus is Coming to Town,"* especially when my little brother and I were cutting up in the car. This song made me wonder, "Is Santa friends with God?" I was extra careful to be good so I wouldn't get the promised bag of switches for bad boys and girls. Our Christmas Eve was spent at my granny's house. There would be a favorite dish for everyone, which is what made her meals special. My favorite part was to stir the coconut pie filling in the double boiler. I have that double boiler to this day, and coconut pie is still my favorite dessert. The memories of being a child on Christmas Eve are precious.

Christmas Lamb

Brenda Montgomery
Lebanon, IN

When my youngest daughter was two, my husband's was the only income and we didn't have much extra for Christmas. So, we put in for a little help from a local group for presents for the kids. On Christmas Eve, they brought us bags of toys and we set out wrapping some of them. The stuffed animals we didn't wrap, but set under the Christmas tree as gifts from Santa Claus. One stuffed lamb was for our two-year-old. She latched onto that lamb, loved it and always had to sleep with it. If it wasn't on her bed, she knew that it had fallen between the bed and wall and would get it, then she would settle down for her bedtime story. All these years later, my daughter has kept that lamb, and now it's in her granddaughter's toy box. The lamb still gets played with, and whenever I see it, it brings back the memories of days gone by.

17

Christmas
for Sharing

Red Cowgirl Boots for Christmas
Kimberly Davis
Abilene, TX

This is my favorite Christmas memory. When I was seven years old, I told my parents I wanted some cowgirl boots. A couple of weeks later, they took my younger sister and me to a western store to try on some boots. I didn't think anything about it. A month later, on Christmas morning there were those beautiful red boots! I was so excited and I was just going on about how Santa knew exactly what I wanted. My sister, who is one year younger than me, said, "Kim, there is no Santa Claus... don't you remember trying these on at the store?" After that, I was heartbroken about Santa, but I still loved those red cowgirl boots! To this day, I love to wear my cowgirl boots.

Mini Bike Santa
Kathy Neuppert-Swanson
Hemet, CA

My brother once played Santa Claus on a mini bike! My mother had Christmas gifts to deliver to some friends, and she and my brother came up with a great idea. Up a ladder to the attic he went to retrieve a Santa suit. He put it on, but something was missing. My mother took out her "frosted" silver wig. He put it on, and it was perfect! Off he went on a Honda 90 mini bike, exclaiming "Ho, ho ho!" throughout the neighborhood. Those receiving the gifts were delighted, and our family witnessed a precious memory in the making. Vroom, vroom, Santa!

Memories
for Sharing

Favorite Christmas Present, Dad is Home

Roberta Bottenfield
Connersville, IN

One Christmas when I was four years old, I woke to find that my father was home. It was wonderful, because he had been gone for almost a year serving in Korea, and no one knew he was returning early. It was really something special for a child who was missing her daddy! My father has been gone now for more than 30 years, but this memory still brings me to happy tears.

Dad, My Favorite Part of Christmas

Monica Britt
Fairdale, WV

My dad loved Christmas more than anyone I have ever met. He loved every minute of it! He'd always start playing Christmas music weeks before Christmas. He loved selecting beautiful Christmas cards to mail to family & friends. He and my brother Phil would string Christmas lights everywhere possible. Mom would wrap the gifts, and we would pile them under the tree. Then, Dad would fry some summer sausage in sweet-and-sour sauce, and we would eat it with cheese and crackers as Christmas movies blared on the television. I'll never forget that wonderful feeling growing up, and knowing that my favorite part of Christmas was always my dad!

Christmas
for Sharing

My Favorite Christmas Store

Delores Lakes
Mansfield, OH

When I was growing up in a small town, one store stood out above the rest. The large windows on the second floor in front, and the side windows facing the street, had enticing displays of all the things every member of the family could want. Everything was so tastefully done and a beauty to behold. The store would be open one night, usually during the middle of the week. Santa would be waiting on the second floor area with a small toy for each child and the parents could shop, knowing their children were happily occupied. It was something we all looked forward to each year. I remember receiving a yellow stuffed kitten. I had that well-loved kitten for years, sleeping with it each night. What happy memories I have of that beautiful store that is no longer there!

The best of all gifts around any Christmas tree:
the presence of a happy family all wrapped up
in each other.

–Burton Hillis

Memories
for Sharing

Christmas Morning

Carol Warnat
British Columbia, Canada

Many years ago when I was six, I can remember Santa brought me a beautiful doll almost identical to an American Girl doll. She had white-blonde hair done up in a bun on top of her head. My mother made a complete wardrobe of clothes for the doll that were packed in a toy chest...suits, jeans, nightgowns that she had made on her treadle sewing machine. I was thrilled! Some of the clothes I have kept for my daughter's dolls, because they were so perfect I could not bear to throw them out. It was also the year when "angel hair" became a popular decoration on Christmas trees. When I crawled under the tree to get my presents, that angel hair went down my back and I was itchy all day. No matter the age, it is all about the magic and love on that Christmas morning.

Grandma's Gifts

Heather Anderson
El Dorado Hills, CA

I always appreciated the Christmas gifts my parents gave me. But one of my all-time favorites was one my grandma gave. There were eight of us grandchildren and she didn't have a lot of money. Grandma sewed each one of us a large stocking, and every year she would fill it with a mixture of homemade and store-bought goodies. In the toe of the stocking, there was always a twenty-dollar bill. I of course loved the twenty-dollar bill, but my favorite thing was finding out what goodies she put in there. Grandma was a stellar baker and cook, so everything she made was yummy!

Christmas
for Sharing

A Christmas Tree for
Mother Nature

Jill Ball
Highland, UT

Every year during the holiday season, we spend a day stringing cereal, cranberries, popcorn, pretzels and anything else edible that we have on hand, making long ropes. We take bagel halves and spread one side with peanut butter and birdseed. Then on Christmas Eve, we trek up to the mountains and decorate a tree for all the animals in the forest...our Mother Nature tree. My parents started this tradition when I was young, and now my sibling and I keep the tradition alive with our children. It's a great way to get out into nature in such a busy season.

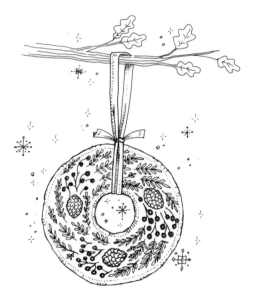

...and heaven and nature sing!
–Christmas carol

Festive Family
Brunch

Christmas
for Sharing

Christmas Morning
Breakfast Casserole

*Ronda Hauss
Bluffton, SC*

When my parents retired to another state, I needed an easy breakfast casserole to serve on Christmas morning during their stays with us. I make it the night before and pop it into the oven first thing on Christmas, before all the lovely craziness begins!

1 lb. ground pork sausage
1/4 c. green onions, chopped
10 slices challah or other white
    bread, torn into pieces
1 c. shredded Cheddar cheese
1 c. shredded Monterey
    Jack cheese

8 eggs, beaten
2-1/2 c. milk
1-1/4 t. dry mustard
1 t. salt
1/2 t. Worcestershire sauce
Garnish: chopped fresh parsley

Cook sausage in a large skillet over medium heat until crumbled and browned, adding onions a few minutes before sausage is done. Drain sausage mixture on a paper towel-lined plate. Meanwhile, spread bread pieces in a 13"x9" baking pan coated with non-stick vegetable spray; sprinkle cheeses evenly over bread. Spoon sausage mixture over cheeses; set aside. In a large bowl, whisk together eggs, milk, mustard, salt and Worcestershire sauce. Pour evenly over sausage mixture. Cover and chill for at least 4 hours, or overnight for best flavor. At least 30 minutes before baking, remove pan from refrigerator and allow it to come to room temperature. Bake, uncovered, at 350 degrees for 45 minutes, or until set. Sprinkle with parsley and serve. Makes 8 servings.

Whether the occasion is shopping day, game day or Christmas morning, make-ahead breakfast casseroles are super time-savers for busy mornings. Assemble the night before, cover and refrigerate, then just pop in the oven...breakfast is served!

Festive Family
Brunch

Peach French Toast

Maureen Charnigo
Medina, OH

This recipe was given to me years ago by my friend Korrine. I've made it for Christmas morning breakfast ever since. Everyone has asked for this recipe once they try it...enjoy!

1 c. brown sugar, packed
1/2 c. butter
2 t. water
29-oz. can sliced peaches,
 drained
12 slices French bread,
 or 6 to 7 slices Texas toast

5 eggs, beaten
1-1/2 c. milk
1 t. vanilla extract
cinnamon to taste

In a saucepan over medium heat, bring brown sugar, butter and water to a boil. Reduce heat to low and simmer for 10 minutes, stirring frequently. Pour into a greased 13"x9" baking pan. Arrange peaches in pan; arrange bread slices over peaches. In a bowl, whisk together eggs, milk and vanilla; pour slowly over bread. Cover and refrigerate for 8 hours or overnight. Remove from refrigerator about 30 minutes before baking; sprinkle with cinnamon. Cover and bake at 350 degrees for 20 minutes. Uncover and bake for 25 to 30 minutes longer, or until bread is golden. Serve with a spoon; recipe makes its own syrup. Serves 6 to 10.

Buttermilk Syrup

Penny Sherman
Ava, MO

This creamy, old-fashioned syrup is scrumptious on waffles and pancakes.

1/2 c. butter
1/2 c. buttermilk
1 c. sugar

1 t. vanilla extract
1 t. baking soda

In a large saucepan over medium heat, melt butter; stir in buttermilk and sugar. Cook over medium heat until mixture starts to boil, about 5 minutes. Remove from heat. Stir in vanilla and baking soda; mixture will foam. Serve immediately. May be covered and refrigerated up to 2 weeks. Makes 6 servings.

Christmas
for Sharing

Grandma Barr's Spiced Coffee Cake

Becky Myers
Ashland, OH

I was lucky to have a grandma who was always willing to teach and share. She raised six children through the Great Depression and always had a smile on her face.

1 c. milk
1 T. lemon juice
2 c. cake flour
2 t. baking powder
2 t. cinnamon
1 t. ground cloves
1/2 t. nutmeg

1/4 t. salt
1 c. sugar
1/2 c. shortening
1/2 t. baking soda
1 egg, beaten
2 T. molasses

Combine milk and lemon juice; set aside until soured. Meanwhile, in a large bowl, sift together flour, baking powder, spices, salt and sugar. Blend in shortening with a pastry blender or fork until pea-size crumbs form. Reserve 1/2 cup crumb mixture for topping. Dissolve baking soda in soured milk; add to remaining flour mixture along with egg and molasses. Stir until smooth. Pour batter into a greased 9"x9" baking pan; spread evenly. Sprinkle with reserved crumb mixture. Bake at 350 degrees for 30 to 40 minutes, until a toothpick inserted in the center comes out clean. Cut into squares. Makes 8 servings.

A cheery, painted chalkboard is ideal for kids as they count down the days until Christmas.

Festive Family
Brunch

Ham & Egg Casserole

Patty Flak
Erie, PA

This breakfast dish is yummy on Christmas morning, or a good way to use the leftover holiday ham! It's very easy to make, too.

6 slices cooked ham, cubed
6 slices bread, cubed
1 c. shredded Swiss or
    other cheese
6 eggs, beaten

2 c. milk
1 t. dried, minced onions
1 t. dry mustard
salt and pepper to taste

In a greased 13"x9" baking pan, combine ham, bread and cheese; set aside. In a large bowl, whisk together remaining ingredients. Pour over ham mixture and stir gently. Bake, uncovered, at 350 degrees for 45 minutes, or until golden and eggs are set. Makes 10 servings.

Holiday Hot Tea

Beckie Apple
Grannis, AR

Cold wintry days and festive get-togethers are the perfect time for this delicious hot tea...it makes the spirits bright!

4 c. boiling water
1 family-size tea bag
64-oz. bottle cranberry
    juice cocktail
1 c. sugar

1 apple, cored and quartered
1 orange, peeled, seeded and
    quartered
2 4-inch cinnamon sticks
1/2 t. ground cloves

Combine boiling water and tea bag in a 4-quart slow cooker. Let stand for 5 minutes; discard tea bag. Add remaining ingredients; stir. Cover and cook on high setting for 2 to 3 hours. Serve hot. Makes 8 to 10 servings.

A countertop mug tree makes a fun display rack for cherished Christmas ornaments.

Christmas
for Sharing

Breakfast Pizza

Sharon Theisen
Saint Cloud, MN

Overnight guests always love this pizza when I serve it for breakfast. It's great any time of day! Use a frozen pizza crust or your own favorite homemade crust.

2 to 3 t. olive oil
1 frozen pizza crust, thawed
6 eggs, beaten
kosher salt and pepper to taste
1-1/2 T. butter
2 c. frozen potato puffs, thawed
   and crumbled

1 c. shredded Cheddar cheese
8 slices bacon, crisply cooked
   and chopped, or 5 brown &
   serve sausage links, browned
   and sliced
Optional: chopped fresh parsley

Drizzle a pizza pan or sheet pan with olive oil; place crust on pan. Bake at 450 degrees for 15 to 20 minutes, until edges are golden; remove from oven. Meanwhile, in a large bowl, whisk together eggs and seasonings. Melt butter in a skillet over medium-low heat. Add egg mixture and cook for 2 to 3 minutes until scrambled, using a spatula to stir eggs from edges to center of pan to form large soft curds. Eggs should be just barely set around the edges. Top baked crust with potato puffs; spread across crust. Top with scrambled eggs, cheese and bacon or sausage. Bake at 450 degrees for 5 minutes, or until cheese melts. If desired, sprinkle with parsley. Cut into wedges. Serves 2 to 4.

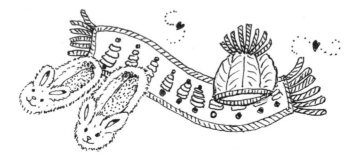

Lots of family members to buy for? Choose a single item like woolly knitted scarves or cozy winter slippers to buy for everyone, in different colors and textures.

Festive Family *Brunch*

Cozy Pancake Bake

Paula Marchesi
Auburn, PA

Quick, easy and delicious! This breakfast is one that I served my family when the boys were growing up. Now, I serve it whenever we have company, and it's still made quite often.

1 lb. ground pork sausage
2 eggs, room temperature, beaten
2 c. biscuit baking mix
1-1/3 c. milk
1/4 c. canola oil

2 apples, peeled, cored and
  thinly sliced
2 T. cinnamon-sugar
Garnish: warm maple syrup

In a large skillet over medium heat, cook and crumble sausage for 5 to 7 minutes, until no longer pink; drain. In a large bowl, whisk together eggs, baking mix, milk and oil until blended; stir in sausage. Transfer batter to a greased 13"x9" baking pan. Top with apples; sprinkle with cinnamon-sugar. Bake at 350 degrees for 30 to 45 minutes, until set and golden. Cut into squares; serve with warm maple syrup. Makes 8 servings.

For extra-special pancakes or French toast, whip up some maple butter in no time. Just blend 1/2 cup butter with 3/4 cup maple syrup...yummy!

Christmas
for Sharing

Blender Pancakes & Strawberry Preserves Syrup

Kathy Grashoff
Fort Wayne, IN

Holidays are busy enough! Get your family started off right with a quick yet delicious breakfast, from your blender.

1 c. milk	1 egg, beaten
1 c. all-purpose flour	2 t. sugar
2 T. oil	1 t. salt

Combine milk and flour in a blender; process for 3 minutes. Add remaining ingredients and process until batter is smooth. Ladle batter by 1/4 cupfuls onto a hot greased skillet; cook until bubbles begin to form. Flip over; cook until done. Serve pancakes with Strawberry Preserves Syrup. Serves 4.

Strawberry Preserves Syrup:

2 c. strawberry preserves	3 T. light corn syrup
1/2 c. water	

Combine all ingredients in a saucepan over low heat. Cook, stirring occasionally, until small bubbles appear around the edges. Simmer for 2 to 3 minutes, stirring occasionally. Serve warm. Makes about 2-1/2 cups.

Don't wait 'til Christmas Day to use your festive holiday dishes... use them all season long for a daily dose of cheer!

Festive Family
Brunch

Cranberry-Pecan Butter

Paula Marchesi
Auburn, PA

Every Christmas, I make this pretty butter. I've been making this since I was a little girl...it's a tasty family tradition. We enjoy it on breakfast pancakes, waffles, muffins and toast, even dinner rolls and crackers. You can use other nuts that you like, such as cashews, walnuts, pistachios or Brazil nuts.

3/4 c. butter, softened
2 T. brown sugar, packed
2 T. light corn syrup

1 c. fresh cranberries, chopped
2 T. toasted chopped pecans

In a bowl, combine butter, sugar and corn syrup. Using a whisk or electric mixer, beat until fluffy, about 5 minutes. Add cranberries and pecans; beat 5 minutes longer, or until mixture turns pink. Transfer to a sheet of plastic wrap; shape into a log, wrap and chill until serving time. Makes about 1-1/3 cups.

Cinnamon Syrup

Jill Ball
Highland, UT

This is a scrumptious syrup. It's perfect for cold wintry mornings. Just drizzle it over waffles, pancakes or French toast.

2 c. sugar
1 c. light corn syrup
1/2 c. water

1 t. cinnamon
5-oz. can evaporated milk

Combine sugar, corn syrup, water and cinnamon in a saucepan over medium heat. Bring to a boil; boil for 2 minutes. Cool for 5 minutes. Stir in evaporated milk; serve warm. Makes 3-3/4 cups.

Enjoy a cozy winter's morning...serve white hot chocolate sprinkled with a dusting of cocoa powder.

Christmas
for Sharing

Toffee-Macadamia Nut
Coffee Cake

Beth Flack
Terre Haute, IN

*Serve this delicious coffee cake on Christmas morning with
hot chocolate and coffee. Also good on a brunch table,
or wrapped up as a gift that's sure to be welcome.*

1-2/3 c. all-purpose flour
3/4 c. brown sugar, packed
1/3 c. butter, softened
1 egg, beaten
1 c. milk

2 t. baking powder
1/2 t. salt
1/4 c. toffee baking bits, divided
1/4 c. flaked coconut
1/4 c. chopped macadamia nuts

In a large bowl, combine flour, brown sugar, butter, egg, milk,
baking powder and salt. Beat with an electric mixer on low speed for
30 seconds. Lower speed to medium and beat for 2 minutes. Stir in
2 tablespoons toffee bits. Pour batter into a greased 9"x9" baking pan.
Sprinkle batter with remaining toffee bits, coconut and nuts. Bake at
350 degrees for 32 to 35 minutes, until a toothpick inserted in the
center comes out clean. Cool completely; cut into squares. Makes
12 servings.

Streamline your holiday plans...just ask your family what
traditions they cherish the most, including favorite cookies
and other festive foods. You can focus on tried & true
activities and free up time to try something new.

Festive Family
Brunch

English Muffin Breakfast Casserole

Jackie Burroughs
Marathon, NY

I love this make-ahead casserole because it's easy...my family loves it because it's delicious! Perfect for brunch get-togethers and Christmas breakfast.

2 12-oz. pkgs. breakfast
   sausage links
6 English muffins, cut into
   1-inch cubes
1/4 c. butter, melted
1 c. shredded Cheddar cheese
1 c. shredded mozzarella cheese
1/2 c. onion, chopped

1/2 c. red pepper, chopped
1 doz. eggs, beaten
2 c. milk
1/4 t. salt
1/4 t. pepper
1/4 c. bacon, crisply cooked
   and crumbled

Cook sausage according to package directions; drain. Cool slightly; slice 1/4-inch thick. In a greased 13"x9" baking pan, layer half each of English muffins and cooked sausage. Repeat layering; drizzle with melted butter. Top with cheeses, onion and red pepper; set aside. In a large bowl, whisk together eggs, milk, salt and pepper; pour over mixture in pan. Sprinkle with bacon. Cover and refrigerate overnight. In the morning, remove from refrigerator 30 minutes before baking. Uncover and bake at 350 degrees for 45 to 50 minutes, until a knife tip inserted in the center comes out clean. Let stand 5 minutes before serving. Makes 10 to 12 servings.

Bring a bit of retro to the holiday kitchen...tie on
a vintage Christmas apron!

Christmas
for Sharing

Hearty Holiday Sausage Muffins

Sherri Ledbetter
Coweta, OK

I'm so excited! I entered a recipe contest sponsored by "Made In Oklahoma" foods and our local television station. My entry was chosen as the winner in the "Most Made-in-Oklahoma Ingredients" category. My recipe was also chosen as the "Top Recipe." Yay! So...on the noon news one day on the "Cooking Corner" segment, they made my recipe. It was really cool to hear my name on TV.

1/2 lb. ground pork sausage
3/4 c. yellow cornmeal
1/4 c. all-purpose flour
1 T. baking powder
1 t. salt
2 eggs, lightly beaten
1 c. sour cream

1/2 c. butter, softened
10-oz. pkg. frozen corn, thawed
1 c. shredded sharp Cheddar
   cheese
1/2 c. red pepper, chopped
1 t. hot pepper sauce, or to taste

Brown sausage in a skillet over medium heat; drain and set aside. Meanwhile, combine cornmeal, flour, baking powder and salt in a large bowl; mix together. Add eggs, sour cream and butter; stir until thoroughly combined. Batter will be light and fluffy. Stir in remaining ingredients. Spoon batter into 18 greased muffin cups, filling almost to the top. Bake at 375 degrees for 15 to 19 minutes, testing for doneness with a toothpick. Remove from oven; let muffins cool in pan for one minute. Remove muffins from pan. Makes 1-1/2 dozen.

Make cranberry, orange or apple juice extra-special
for holiday mornings...just add a splash of ginger ale.

Festive Family *Brunch*

Omelet Waffles

Carolyn Deckard
Bedford, IN

This great breakfast waffle was one of our favorites that
my mom made on Sunday mornings before going to church.

4 eggs, separated
1/4 c. all-purpose flour
6 T. hot water
2 T. butter, melted

1/2 t. salt
1/8 t. pepper
2 T. fresh parsley, chopped

In a large bowl, beat egg whites with an electric mixer on high speed until stiff peaks form; set aside. In another bowl, beat egg yolks until light in color; set aside. In a third bowl, combine flour, hot water, butter, salt and pepper; beat until smooth and add to egg yolks. Fold in egg whites and parsley. Ladle by 1/2 cupfuls onto a hot greased waffle iron; bake for 2 minutes. Makes 4 waffles.

Glazed Breakfast Sausages

Laura Fuller
Fort Wayne, IN

So easy to make...they really dress up a breakfast plate!

12 brown & serve sausages
1 c. pure maple syrup

1/2 c. brown sugar, packed
1 t. cinnamon

Brown sausages in a skillet according to package directions; drain. Combine remaining ingredients in a small bowl; blend well and spoon over sausages. Cook over low heat until sausages are well coated, stirring gently. Serves 6.

Just for fun, set out snowman-
shaped candy marshmallows
for folks to float in their hot cocoa!

Christmas
for Sharing

Christmas Morning Scones

Judy Gillham
Whittier, CA

Our family has always enjoyed the simplicity of a quiet Christmas morning, with presents to open, coffee and a delicious batch of scones warm from the oven. This recipe can be prepared the night before, kept in the fridge to keep the butter cold, then formed and finished in a few minutes. Pop it the oven while the coffee brews.

2-1/2 c. all-purpose flour
1 T. baking powder
1/2 t. salt
8 T. cold butter
1/3 c. sugar

2/3 c. whole milk
Garnish: additional milk
    or beaten egg, sugar or
    cinnamon-sugar

In a large bowl, whisk together flour, baking powder and salt. Cut in butter with a pastry blender or 2 knives until mixture looks like coarse crumbs. Add sugar; toss with a fork to mix. Add milk; stir with a fork until dough forms. Gather dough into a ball and turn out onto a floured surface. Gently pat or roll out dough into a circle, about 1/2 inch thick. Cut dough into wedges or circles as desired. Place scones on an ungreased baking sheet, slightly apart for crisp edges. Lightly brush tops with milk or beaten egg; sprinkle with sugar or cinnamon-sugar. Bake at 425 degrees for about 12 minutes, until golden. Serve scones hot from the oven. Makes 6 scones.

Variations:

Cranberry-Orange Scones: Soak a small handful of dried cranberries in hot water; drain. Add cranberries and zest of one orange after mixing in the sugar.

May divide dough into 2 balls to form 2 circles; this will result in smaller scones and more servings.

Cookie cutters make sweet wreath or garland tie-ons.

Festive Family
Brunch

Santa's Favorite French Toast

Jill Ball
Highland, UT

I use this recipe not only for Christmas morning, but anytime we have guests staying with us. It's a sweet way to start the day without a lot of fuss. It's also one of Santa's favorites!

1 loaf French bread, cut into
    1-inch slices on the diagonal
8 eggs, beaten
2 c. milk
1-1/2 c. half-and-half

2 t. vanilla extract
1/4 t. cinnamon
3/4 c. butter
1-1/3 c. brown sugar, packed
3 T. light corn syrup

Arrange bread slices in the bottom of a buttered 13"x9" baking pan; set aside. In a large bowl, beat together eggs, milk, half-and-half, vanilla and cinnamon. Pour over bread slices; cover and refrigerate overnight. The next morning, preheat oven to 350 degrees. In a small saucepan, combine butter, brown sugar and corn syrup; cook and stir until bubbly and brown sugar is dissolved. Pour over bread and egg mixture. Bake, uncovered, at 350 degrees for 40 minutes, until set and golden. Makes 10 to 12 servings.

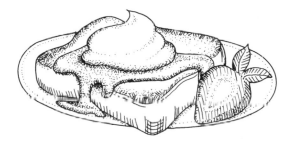

Whip up a luscious topping to dollop on waffles and French toast. Combine 3/4 cup whipping cream, 2 tablespoons softened cream cheese and one tablespoon powdered sugar. Beat with an electric mixer on medium speed until soft peaks form. Keep refrigerated in a small covered crock.

Kolacky

Nan Wysock
New Port Richey, FL

This recipe is from Europe. It is a favorite with my family and the friends I have shared these delicious nut rolls with. We enjoy them at breakfast with hot chocolate.

2 envs. active dry yeast
1 c. warm milk, about 110 to
    115 degrees
8 c. all-purpose flour, divided

2 T. sugar
1 t. salt
8 egg yolks, beaten and divided
1 lb. butter

For first dough: In a large bowl, dissolve yeast in warm milk; let stand for 5 minutes. Add 4 cups flour, sugar, salt and half of beaten egg yolks; mix well and set aside. For second dough: In another large bowl, work butter into remaining flour until it has the consistency of cornmeal. Combine both doughs and mix well. Place dough in a lightly greased bowl; cover and let rise for 2 hours. Punch down; let rise another 2 hours. Sprinkle a pastry sheet with powdered sugar; roll out half of dough into a rectangle, 1/2-inch thick. Spread dough with half of Nut Filling; roll up jelly-roll style, sealing edges. Place roll seam-side down on a parchment paper-lined baking sheet. Repeat with remaining dough and filling; brush rolls with remaining beaten egg yolks. Bake at 350 degrees for 30 minutes. Cool on a wire rack; slice rolls to serve. Baked rolls may be frozen for one to 2 months. Makes 2 rolls, 8 servings each.

Nut Filling:

8 egg whites
2 c. sugar
2 t. vanilla extract

1-1/2 lbs. pecans or walnuts,
    chopped or ground

In a large bowl, beat egg whites with an electric mixer on high speed until soft peaks form. Beat in sugar and vanilla; fold in nuts.

It is Christmas in the heart
that puts Christmas in the air.
–W.T. Ellis

Festive Family
Brunch

Camper's Hot Chocolate Mix

Bethi Hendrickson
Danville, PA

This recipe was part of a wedding gift from my sweet friend Shirley. It's a great recipe for giving as a gift with some cute mugs, tiny marshmallows and a pack of holiday sprinkles.

25.6-oz. jar non-fat dry milk
16-oz. can hot chocolate mix
6-oz. jar powdered non-dairy
    creamer

4-3/4 c. powdered sugar, sifted
Garnish: tiny marshmallows,
    candy sprinkles

Combine all ingredients in a large container; mix thoroughly. Store in a tightly covered container; attach directions. Directions: for one serving, combine 3/4 cup hot water and 1/4 cup hot chocolate mix; stir well. Garnish as desired. Makes 15 cups mix, about 60 servings.

Christmas Coffee

Anna McMaster
Portland, OR

Who doesn't love a cup of hot coffee, spiced up for the holidays?

10 c. hot brewed coffee
1/2 c. sugar
1/4 c. baking cocoa
1/4 t. cinnamon

1/3 c. water
Garnish: whipped cream,
    milk, sugar

Pour hot coffee into a serving pitcher; cover and set aside. In a saucepan over medium heat, combine sugar, cocoa, cinnamon and water. Bring to a boil; boil for one minute, stirring frequently. Add to coffee; stir and serve immediately, garnished as desired. Stir again if served later. Makes 8 to 10 servings.

Christmas
for Sharing

Mother's Christmas Fruit Salad

Jackie Garvin
Valrico, FL

This simple fruit salad was always the star of Mother's Christmas table. In her eyes, a celebration at our house wouldn't be complete without a good fruit salad! She'd carefully select the fruit and make sure she had the best she could find, changing the fruit according to the season. On Christmas, Mother dressed up the salad with shredded coconut and chopped pecans. The acid in the orange juice will help keep the bananas and apples from turning brown.

3 whole oranges, divided
1 T. honey, or to taste
1 qt. strawberries, hulled
   and chopped
1 bunch seedless red grapes,
   halved

2 bananas, sliced
2 Gala apples, peeled if desired,
   cored and chopped

Squeeze the juice from one orange; mix juice with honey and set aside. Peel and chop remaining 2 oranges; place oranges in a large bowl. Add strawberries, grapes, bananas and apples. (May peel one apple and leave the other unpeeled for added color, texture and flavor.) Drizzle orange juice mixture over fruit. Gently stir to make sure all the fruit is coated. Cover and chill until serving time. Makes 8 to 10 servings.

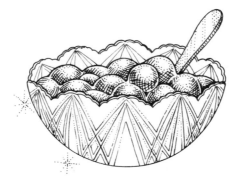

The bright colors of fresh fruit really shine in an antique cut-glass bowl. When washing cut glass, add a little white vinegar to the rinse water...the glass will really sparkle!

Festive Family *Brunch*

Baked Chicken Salad in Crust

Lisa Gowen
Saint Charles, MO

I needed a brunch-type main dish for an occasion,
and a girlfriend shared this recipe with me. It was a hit!

9-inch deep-dish pie crust,
    unbaked
2 eggs
1/2 c. cream of chicken soup
1/2 c. sour cream
1/2 c. mayonnaise
2 T. all-purpose flour

2 t. salt
2 c. cooked chicken, diced
1/2 c. shredded Cheddar cheese
1/2 c. celery, finely chopped
1/4 c. water chestnuts, finely
    chopped

Pierce pie crust lightly with a fork. Bake at 350 degrees for 7 to
10 minutes; set aside. Meanwhile, lightly beat eggs in a large bowl.
Add chicken soup, sour cream, mayonnaise, flour and salt; mix well.
Fold in chicken, cheese, celery and water chestnuts. Spoon mixture into
baked crust. Bake at 350 degrees for 60 to 70 minutes, until filling is
firm in the center and crust is lightly golden. Cut into wedges. Makes
6 servings.

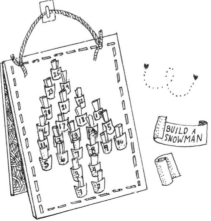

An Advent calendar helps the days pass for eager kids! Create your
own with pictures clipped from old Christmas cards. Behind each
door, write a quick fun-to-do idea, like "Make a paper chain" or
"Feed the birds" or "Write a letter to Santa." Every day at
breakfast, you can share the day's activity together.

Christmas
for Sharing

Overnight Apple Oatmeal with Brown Sugar Streusel

Leona Krivda
Belle Vernon, PA

*I made this oatmeal for my family's Christmas morning breakfast...
it was a big hit! I served it with fresh blueberries, dried cranberries,
slivered almonds, more brown sugar and warm milk. It's not only easy
to make ahead, it's so good I think even Santa would like it!*

4 T. butter, divided
4 c. cooking apples, peeled, cored
    and chopped
3/4 c. plus 2 T. brown sugar,
    packed
1 t. cinnamon
1/3 c. apple cider
2 c. milk
1 c. chunky applesauce

2 eggs, beaten
1 T. cinnamon
1/2 t. nutmeg
1/2 t. salt
2 t. vanilla extract
3 c. old-fashioned oats,
    uncooked
1 c. steel-cut oats, uncooked

Melt 2 tablespoons butter in a large skillet over medium heat; add
apples, 2 tablespoons brown sugar and cinnamon. Stir to coat well;
add cider. Cook for 10 to 15 minutes, until apples are soft and cider is
mostly cooked down. Remove from heat; set aside. Meanwhile, in a
large bowl, whisk together milk, applesauce, eggs, seasonings, vanilla
and remaining melted butter and brown sugar. Stir in apples and
old-fashioned oats; stir in steel-cut oats. Spread evenly in a buttered
9"x9" baking pan. Cover tightly with plastic wrap, pressing it directly
onto the surface. Refrigerate overnight. In the morning, uncover; top
with Streusel mixture. Bake at 375 degrees for 30 to 35 minutes, until
hot and streusel is golden. Serve warm. Makes 6 to 8 servings.

Streusel:

1/3 c. all-purpose flour
1/3 c. old-fashioned oats,
    uncooked
1/3 c. brown sugar, packed

1/2 t. baking powder
1/2 t. salt
4 T. butter, cut into 1/2-inch
    pieces, room temperature

Combine all ingredients except butter in a bowl; stir together with a fork.
Cut in butter with fork until large pea-size crumbs form. If making
ahead, cover and set aside at room temperature. Do not add to oat
mixture until baking time in the morning.

Festive Family *Brunch*

Country Skillet

Gladys Kielar
Whitehouse, OH

This tasty recipe can be ready in 30 minutes! It's equally good for breakfast or dinner.

6 slices bacon
6 c. frozen diced potatoes,
    thawed
3/4 c. red pepper, chopped
1/2 c. onion, chopped

1 t. salt
1/4 t. pepper
6 eggs, beaten
1/2 c. shredded Cheddar cheese

Cook bacon in a large cast-iron skillet over medium heat until crisp. Remove bacon to drain on paper towels; crumble and set aside. Partially drain drippings from skillet. Add potatoes, red pepper, onion, salt and pepper to drippings; cook and stir for 2 minutes. Cover and cook for about 15 minutes, stirring occasionally, until potatoes are tender and golden. Use a spoon to make 6 wells in potato mixture; break one egg into each well. Cover and cook over low heat for 8 to 10 minutes, until eggs are set to desired doneness. Top with cheese and crumbled bacon. Makes 6 servings.

Get out Grandma's cast-iron skillet to cook up crisp, golden breakfast dishes from start to finish, with a touch of love from Grandma. When it's done, set the skillet on a hot pad and serve piping hot, right from the skillet.

Christmas
for Sharing

Melt-in-Your-Mouth Pecan Rolls
Marsha Baker
Pioneer, OH

If you keep refrigerated crescent rolls on hand, you can easily make this luscious dish whenever anyone drops in for coffee. It's so very good. I have cut back on the sugar amount just a tad. Don't make them when you're at home by yourself...it's too tempting!

1/4 c. plus 3 T. butter, melted
    and divided
1/4 c. brown sugar, packed
1 T. light corn syrup
1/3 c. chopped pecans

1/4 c. sugar
1 t. cinnamon
8-oz. tube refrigerated
    crescent rolls

Spread 1/4 cup melted butter in an 8"x 8" baking pan; stir in brown sugar. Add corn syrup and blend well. Sprinkle with pecans; set aside. Add remaining butter to a shallow dish; combine sugar and cinnamon in another dish. Unroll crescent rolls and cut into 16 equal pieces. Dip each slice into melted melted butter, then into cinnamon-sugar. Arrange slices cut-side down on top of brown sugar mixture, making 4 rows of 4. Bake at 375 degrees for 13 to 17 minutes, until golden. Cool in pan for one minute before inverting onto a serving plate. Makes 16 rolls.

Breakfast with Santa...what fun! Ask a family friend to play Santa for the children at your holiday brunch. They'll love sharing secrets with the jolly old elf over waffles and hot cocoa.

Festive Family
Brunch

Fruit Pancake Muffins

Shirley Lafferty
Beloit, KS

A family favorite. Easy to make & enjoy...smiles all around! Soft fruits like bananas, berries and peaches work well in this recipe.

2 c. biscuit baking mix
2 eggs, beaten
1 c. milk
1/2 c. club soda

1 T. oil
1 c. fresh fruit, diced
1/4 c. pancake syrup

In a large bowl, combine baking mix, eggs, milk, club soda and oil; mix well. Pour batter into 12 sprayed muffin cups; sprinkle with fruit. Bake at 350 degrees for 20 to 25 minutes, until a toothpick comes out clean. Remove muffins from pan; brush tops with syrup. Serve warm. Makes one dozen.

Easy Eggnog

Teresa Verell
Roanoke, VA

Everyone always enjoys this eggnog! My family serves it at the Thanksgiving and Christmas holidays.

7 c. 2% milk, divided
3.4-oz. pkg. French vanilla
   instant pudding mix

2 T. sugar
1 t. vanilla extract
1 c. evaporated milk

Combine 2 cups 2% milk, dry pudding mix, sugar and vanilla in a large bowl; whisk together for 2 minutes. Pour mixture into a half-gallon container with a tight-fitting lid. Add 3 cups 2% milk; shake well. Add evaporated milk and shake. Add remaining 2% milk; shake well. Cover and chill for 8 hours before serving. Makes 8 servings.

Set out peppermint sticks for stirring
breakfast cocoa...it's Christmas!

Christmas
for Sharing

Constance's Family Quiche

*Constance Bockstoce
Dallas, GA*

Holidays are full of rich foods. This recipe has the taste of a rich quiche, yet it's healthier and lighter. Not wanting a thick crust and wanting an easy fix for the crust, I opted to use a sandwich wrap. Now it's all I use when I make quiche.

1 lb. ground pork sausage
2 c. broccoli slaw
1 c. frozen diced pepper &
   onion mix
1 t. garlic powder
1 to 2 t. oil
2 large sun-dried tomato
   sandwich wraps

8 eggs, beaten
1-1/3 c. evaporated milk
1/3 c. light sour cream
1/2 c. grated Parmesan cheese
pepper to taste

In a non-stick skillet over medium heat, cook sausage until no longer pink; drain. Add broccoli slaw and frozen pepper & onion mix; sprinkle with garlic powder. Cook for about 10 minutes, stirring often, until tender. Remove from heat. Lightly brush 2, 9" pie plates with oil; press a sandwich wrap into each pie plate. Spoon half of sausage mixture into each pie plate, covering the bottoms; do not press down. Set aside. In a bowl, whisk together remaining ingredients. Pour half of egg mixture into each pie plate. Bake at 375 degrees for 30 to 40 minutes, until set. Cut into wedges; serve warm. Makes 2 quiches; each serves 4 to 6.

Add whimsical patterns, pictures and holiday greetings to plain glass ball ornaments with colorful paint pens from the craft store. So pretty on the Christmas tree...perfect as placecards, too!

Festive Family
Brunch

Pecan Pancakes

Marsha Baker
Pioneer, OH

Fluffy and oh-so flavorful, these are a terrific treat...a copycat recipe from a favorite country-style restaurant.

2 c. all-purpose flour
1 t. baking soda
1 t. salt
1 T. sugar

2 c. buttermilk
1 egg, beaten
3/4 to 1 c. chopped pecans
Garnish: warm maple syrup

In a large bowl, combine flour, baking soda, salt and sugar; mix well. Add buttermilk; stir well. Blend in egg just until mixed. Pour batter onto a hot greased griddle by 1/3 cupfuls; sprinkle pecans over batter. Cook until golden on the bottom and bubbles appear around the edges; flip and cook the other side. Serve hot with warm maple syrup. Makes 8 to 10 servings.

Orange Biscuits

Angie Salayon
New Orleans, LA

Wonderful biscuits with an orange surprise!

1 c. powdered sugar
1/3 c. butter, softened
zest and juice of 1 large
  navel orange

10-oz. tube refrigerated flaky
  biscuits, separated

In a bowl, mix together powdered sugar, butter and orange zest. Slowly stir in enough orange juice to moisten well. Form mixture into 10 balls; place one ball in the center of each biscuit. Form each biscuit into a ball around powdered sugar mixture; press lightly to seal. Arrange biscuits on a buttered baking sheet, sealed side down. Bake at 400 degrees for 8 to 11 minutes, until golden. Makes 10 biscuits.

Keep a sugar shaker handy for dusting powdered sugar
onto waffles, biscuits and cookies.

Christmas
for Sharing

Homemade Waffles

Donna Wilson
Maryville, TN

*This is my favorite go-to recipe for my favorite waffle maker.
My kids have always loved my "Mickey" waffles!*

1-3/4 c. all-purpose flour
2 T. sugar
1 t. baking powder
1/2 t. baking soda
1/2 t. salt

2 eggs, beaten
2 c. buttermilk
1/2 c. oil
1 t. vanilla extract
Garnish: butter, pancake syrup

In a bowl, mix together flour, sugar, baking powder, baking soda and salt; set aside. In a separate bowl, whisk together eggs, buttermilk, oil and vanilla. Add flour mixture to egg mixture; stir well. Add batter by 1/4 to 1/2 cupfuls to a preheated, greased waffle maker; bake according to manufacture's directions. Spread with butter; serve with syrup as desired. Serves 4.

Serve up waffles with sundae fixin's...sure to become a new Christmas morning tradition. Top warm, flaky waffles with vanilla ice cream, chocolate syrup and a dollop of whipped cream...and don't forget the cherry!

Festive Family *Brunch*

Baked Pineapple

Hannah Thiry
Luxemburg, WI

This pineapple is so, so good on French toast, waffles and pancakes. You can even serve it over ice cream...awesome!

3 T. butter, softened
1 c. light brown sugar, loosely
    packed and divided
juice of one orange

2/3 c. bourbon or pineapple juice
1 pineapple, peeled, cored and
    cut into 8 rings

Spread butter in the bottom of a 13"x9" baking pan; sprinkle with half of brown sugar. Drizzle orange juice and bourbon or pineapple juice all over brown sugar. Arrange pineapple rings on top; sprinkle with remaining brown sugar. Set pan on bottom oven rack. Bake at 375 degrees for about 50 minutes, occasionally spooning pan juices over pineapple and turning the rings once or twice, until tender and glazed. If pineapple is tender, but pan juices are still too runny, pour off juices into a skillet and simmer over low heat until reduced, while keeping pineapple warm in the oven. Makes 8 servings.

The children were nestled all snug in their beds,
While visions of sugarplums danced in their heads.
–Clement Moore

Christmas
for Sharing

Beckie's Bread Pudding

Beckie Apple
Grannis, AR

Bread pudding is one of our favorite desserts and it's so easy to make. I like to bake it ahead of time, then serve it for breakfast with warm pancake syrup. Yum!

4 eggs, beaten
2-3/4 c. whole milk
1-3/4 c. sugar
2 t. vanilla extract

1/2 c. chopped pecans or
   English walnuts
6 c. crusty day-old bread, French
   bread or biscuits, cubed

In a large bowl, combine eggs, milk, sugar and vanilla; beat until sugar is well dissolved. Add nuts and stir well. Add bread cubes; push down into egg mixture and gently toss to soak well. Spoon mixture into a 9"x9" deep baking pan coated with non-stick vegetable spray. Bake at 350 degrees for 30 to 35 minutes, until a knife tip inserted in the center comes out clean. Drizzle Sauce over warm bread pudding and serve. Makes 6 servings.

Sauce:

1-3/4 c. powered sugar
1/4 c. warm water

1 t. vanilla extract

Combine all ingredients; mix with a fork until smooth.

Fill a basket with little bags of "Reindeer Food" for kids to sprinkle on the lawn on Christmas Eve. To make, simply mix cereal rings with candy sprinkles. They'll love it!

Festive Family
Brunch

Christmas Cranberry Coffee Cake

Diana Krol
Hutchinson, KS

This coffee cake forms its own glaze and needs no additional icing. Quick and delicious, it's especially nice to serve during the holidays when fresh cranberries are available. I like to tuck several packages of cranberries in the freezer for later.

3 eggs, beaten
2 c. sugar
3/4 c. butter
2 t. vanilla extract

2 c. all-purpose flour
12-oz. pkg. fresh or frozen
    cranberries

Combine eggs and sugar in a large bowl. Beat with an electric mixer on medium-high speed for 7 minutes, until thickened and yellow. Add butter and vanilla; beat for 2 additional minutes. Stir in flour and mix until just combined. Gently stir in cranberries, blending well. Pour batter into a lightly greased 12"x9" baking pan. Bake at 350 degrees for 40 to 50 minutes, testing for doneness with a toothpick. Cut into squares; serve warm or cooled. Makes 8 to 10 servings.

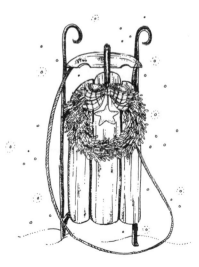

Old-fashioned favorites like a vintage sled or pair of ice skates by the front door are a sweet welcome for friends. Tie on evergreen boughs and red berry sprigs for cheery color.

Christmas
for Sharing

Hashbrown Bake

Delores Lakes
Mansfield, OH

A friend made this tasty recipe for a group she was hosting. Everyone loved it and several asked her for the recipe. It's sure to be welcome at both brunch and dinner.

2 12-oz. pkgs. frozen diced
   hashbrown potatoes
16-oz. container sour cream
10-3/4 oz. can cream of
   chicken soup

10-oz. pkg. shredded sharp
   Cheddar cheese
2 c. corn flake cereal, crushed
1/2 c. butter, melted

In a large bowl, combine all ingredients except cereal and melted butter; mix well. Spread evenly in a greased 13"x9" baking pan. Toss together cereal and melted butter in another bowl; spread on top. Bake, uncovered, at 350 degrees for one hour, or until bubbly and golden. Serves 8.

Lisa's Bacon Gravy

Lisa Green
Parkersburg, WV

I make this delicious gravy on the weekends for my husband. It's delicious spooned over biscuits or toast...enjoy!

4 slices bacon
1 T. all-purpose flour
1/4 t. pepper

1 c. milk
1/2 t. less-sodium soy sauce

Cook bacon in a large skillet over medium heat until crisp; drain on paper towels. Drain skillet, reserving one tablespoon drippings. Add flour and pepper to reserved drippings. Cook over medium heat for one to 2 minutes, stirring often, until hot and bubbly. Gradually whisk in milk until blended; stir in soy sauce. Cook over medium heat for 3 to 4 minutes, stirring constantly, or just until gravy thickens and comes to a boil. Serve hot; garnish with crumbled bacon if desired. Makes 4 servings.

Merry-Making
Appetizers

Christmas
for Sharing

Green Chile Tortilla Pinwheels

Jenna Harmon
Dolores, CO

My mother-in-law started making this recipe for special holidays and events back in the early 1990s. When he was growing up, it became one of my husband's favorites, so she passed the recipe to me. Now I always bring it to celebrations, holiday gatherings and potlucks. The guests empty the platter quickly every time and they always ask for the recipe.

8-oz. container sour cream
8-oz. pkg. cream cheese,
   softened
4-oz. can chopped black olives,
   drained

4-oz. can diced green chiles
1/2 c. green onions, chopped
1 c. shredded Mexican-blend
   cheese
4 to 5 large flour tortillas

In a large bowl, combine all ingredients except tortillas; blend together well. Spread mixture evenly over each tortilla. Roll up tortillas and cut into one-inch slices; arrange pinwheels on a platter. Cover with plastic wrap and refrigerate for a few hours before serving. Makes about 3 dozen.

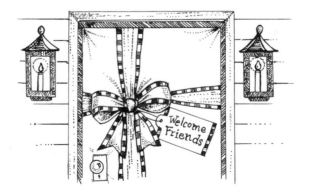

Let your house say a hearty "Merry Christmas" to visitors and passersby! Wrap the front door with brightly colored paper and ribbon like a giant gift package.

Merry-Making
Appetizers

Super Nachos

Vicki Van Donselaar
Cedar, IA

After a large lunch on Christmas, our family enjoys having just appetizers in the evening. This is often requested for our Christmas appetizer meal. It's a tried & true recipe and everyone loves it. Be sure to have plenty of tortilla chips on hand!

16-oz. can refried beans
1 lb. ground beef, browned
    and drained
15-oz. jar salsa con queso
1 c. favorite salsa

1 c. shredded Cheddar cheese
tortilla chips
Garnish: shredded lettuce, sour
    cream, chopped tomatoes,
    peppers, onion

Spread refried beans in an ungreased 11"x9" glass baking pan; layer with browned beef. Add desired amount of salsa con queso; top with salsa and cheese as desired. Bake, uncovered, at 350 degrees for about 20 to 25 minutes, until hot and bubbly. Serve with tortilla chips, garnished as desired. Serves 15 to 20.

Christmastime is a fun-filled, magical time of year...build a snowman, go sledding, even try ice skating! A wintry bonfire with food, family & friends will make it a time to remember.

Christmas
for Sharing

Chicken Cordon Bleu Dip

Lori Murphy
Waukesha, WI

*I love chicken cordon bleu, so this dip is a great favorite.
Serve it warm in a small crock, or double the recipe and
put it in a slow cooker set on warm.*

2 8-oz. pkgs. cream cheese
   softened
1 c. bacon, crisply cooked and
   chopped
1 c. deli rotisserie chicken,
   chopped

1 c. cooked ham, diced
1/4 c. chicken broth
1-1/2 c. shredded Swiss cheese,
   divided
bread cubes or crackers

In a large bowl, combine all ingredients except bread cubes or crackers, reserving 1/4 cup Swiss cheese for topping. Spread evenly in a greased 8"x8" baking pan; sprinkle with reserved cheese. Bake, uncovered, at 350 degrees for 20 to 25 minutes. Serve with bread cubes or crackers. Makes 6 to 8 servings.

Easy Cheesy Cheese Spread

Barbara Jahnke
Lombard, IL

*Only four ingredients and super easy. I get many requests for
this recipe because everyone loves it! Serve with crackers of
your choice. It is best the next day.*

8-oz. pkg. sharp Cheddar
   cheese, cubed
8-oz. pkg. cream cheese,
   softened

1/2 c. butter
2/3 to 1 c. Rhine wine, other
   white wine or low-sodium
   chicken broth

In a small food processor, combine Cheddar cheese chunks; process until chunks are small. Add cream cheese, butter and 2/3 cup wine or broth. Process to a smooth consistency, adding additional wine or broth as needed. Spoon into a lidded container and serve immediately, or for best flavor, cover and refrigerate overnight. Serves 8 or more.

Merry-Making
Appetizers

Buffalo Chicken Dip

Marian Forck
Chamois, MO

This is a good dip to serve at parties, or serve with chips, crackers or fresh veggies and you have an easy meal. I put it in a slow cooker to take to parties and keep on low, stirring occasionally.

2 8-oz. pkgs. cream cheese,
    softened
2 8-oz. cans shredded chicken
    breast, drained
1 c. ranch salad dressing

1/2 to 3/4 c. buffalo wing sauce,
    to taste
8-oz. pkg. shredded Cheddar
    cheese

In a lightly greased 13"x9" baking pan, mix together all ingredients except shredded cheese. Spread cheese on top. Bake, uncovered, at 350 degrees for 15 to 20 minutes, stirring in cheese as it starts to melt. Serves 10 to 12.

Bacon-Swiss Dip

Karen Wilson
Defiance, OH

Bacon and Swiss cheese is one of my favorite combinations! This easy dip is scrumptious with crackers.

8-oz. pkg. cream cheese,
    softened
1 c. shredded Swiss cheese
1/2 c. mayonnaise

2 T. green onions, finely chopped
8 slices bacon, crisply cooked
    and crumbled
assorted crackers

Combine cheeses and mayonnaise in a bowl; mix until combined. Stir in onions and bacon. Spread in a lightly greased 13"x9" shallow baking pan. Bake, uncovered, at 350 degrees for 15 to 20 minutes, until bubbly. Serve hot with assorted crackers. Makes 4 servings.

Cover party tables with giftwrap...done in a jiffy,
and easy toss afterwards.

Christmas
for Sharing

Sheet Pan Butter Shrimp Dijon

Joslyn Hornstrom
Elgin, IL

This tasty shrimp is a family request every holiday, and it's oh-so easy to make. Serve with crusty bread to sop up the sauce. I usually make a double batch, hoping for leftovers to be served over hot cooked pasta the next day.

2 whole lemons, divided
1 c. butter
2 to 3 T. Dijon mustard
2 to 3 cloves garlic, minced
1/4 t. salt, or to taste
1/4 t. white pepper, or to taste

2 lbs. uncooked jumbo shrimp, thawed if frozen, shelled and deveined, tails attached
1 T. fresh parsley, chopped
sliced crusty bread

Slice one lemon and set aside; squeeze 3 tablespoons juice from remaining lemon. In a small saucepan over medium heat, whisk together butter, mustard, reserved lemon juice, garlic, salt and pepper just until butter melts. Remove from heat and let cool to warm. On an ungreased baking sheet, arrange shrimp in a single layer. Spoon butter mixture over shrimp; stir to coat completely. Lay lemon slices on top. Bake, uncovered, at 400 degrees for 12 to 17 minutes, until shrimp is pink and opaque, stirring halfway through. Transfer to a serving dish and sprinkle with parsley; serve with crusty bread. Makes 10 to 12 servings.

It's fun to hang little unexpected surprises from the
dining room chandelier. Start with a swag of greenery,
then tuck in Christmas whimsies like glass balls,
tiny snowmen, cookie cutters and smiling Santas.

Merry-Making
Appetizers

Mushroom Toast

Paula Thessen
Worton, MD

I first started making this tasty recipe years ago with my children when they were little, because they liked to help. You can use white button mushrooms, or a variety of mushrooms.

1 T. butter
8-oz. pkg. sliced mushrooms
2 t. soy sauce
8-oz. pkg. cream cheese,
   softened
1 t. dried parsley

1 t. onion powder
1 t. garlic powder
1 t. Italian seasoning
1/2 c. grated Parmesan cheese
1 French baguette, sliced into
   1/4-inch rounds

Melt butter in a skillet over medium-high heat. Add mushrooms and sauté until nearly tender. Stir in soy sauce; simmer over medium-low heat for 10 minutes. Add cream cheese and seasonings; stir until smooth. Remove from heat; stir in Parmesan cheese. Top each baguette slice with a spoonful of mushroom mixture. Arrange on an ungreased baking sheet. Bake at 350 degrees for 8 to 10 minutes, until crisp and golden. Makes 10 servings.

Invite neighbors over for an afternoon holiday get-together. Serve lots of easy-to-make appetizers and hot spiced cider. Keeping it casual and fuss-free means you'll have lots of time to catch up on each other's holiday plans.

Christmas
for Sharing

Layered Crabmeat Pizza

Debby Marcum
New Castle, IN

This fun and tasty spread is always a hit at any party!

1-1/2 c. cream cheese, softened
1 T. mayonnaise
1 T. Worcestershire sauce
1 T. onion, chopped
1 t. lemon juice
1/8 t. garlic powder

12-oz. bottle chili sauce,
 to taste
16-oz. can crabmeat, drained
 and flaked
Garnish: chopped fresh parsley
hearty crackers

In a large bowl, blend cream cheese, mayonnaise, Worcestershire sauce, onion, lemon juice and garlic powder. Spread mixture evenly on a round serving platter. Spoon desired amount of chili sauce over cheese mixture. Spread crabmeat over chili sauce; sprinkle lightly with parsley. Cover and chill until serving time. Serve with hearty crackers. Makes 6 to 8 servings.

Have an appetizer swap with 3 or 4 friends. Each makes a big batch of a favorite dip, spread or finger food, then get together to sample and divide them up. You'll all have a super variety of goodies for holiday parties.

Merry-Making
Appetizers

Dilled Shrimp Dip

Rosemary Lightbown
Wakefield, RI

Our oldest daughter, who is now in her 40s, has always requested this dip since she was a young girl! I smile every time I make it, knowing it is one of her favorites. If you like, use chopped, fresh-cooked shrimp rather than canned shrimp.

8-oz. pkg. cream cheese,
   softened
1/4 c. milk
1 t. Worcestershire sauce
1 t. lemon juice
1/2 t. dried dill weed

1/2 t. garlic salt
6-oz. can medium shrimp,
   drained, rinsed and chopped
scoop-type or horn-shaped
   corn chips

In a bowl, blend cream cheese and milk. Stir in Worcestershire sauce, lemon juice and seasonings; fold in shrimp. Cover and refrigerate at least one hour. Serve with corn chips. Makes one to 2 cups.

Holiday Cranberry Punch

Eileen Bennett
Jenison, MI

We entertain often during the holidays, and a punch bowl adds a festive touch. Over many years, this blend of ingredients was the most requested and a true family favorite. So pretty...so refreshing!

3-oz. pkg. cherry gelatin mix
1 c. boiling water
6-oz. can frozen lemonade
   concentrate
3 c. cold water

32-oz. bottle cranberry juice
   cocktail
2-ltr. bottle ginger ale, chilled
1 qt. cranberry sherbet

In a large pitcher, mix first 5 ingredients in order given; cover and chill. Just before serving, pour mixture into a punch bowl. Add ginger ale, pouring slowly down the side of bowl; add scoops of sherbet and serve. Makes 25 servings.

The perfect Christmas tree?
All Christmas trees are perfect!
–Charles N. Barnard

Charcuterie Board
Marinated Cheese

Shelly McBeth
Topeka, KS

My family has been doing meat & cheese trays for many years. Now the trays have a fancy name, but we just love having a tray of meats and cheeses for snacking on Christmas Eve and our usual New Year's Eve game night. These cheese cubes are a great addition!

1/3 c. olive oil
1 T. sun-dried tomatoes in oil,
    drained
1 T. fresh parsley, minced
1 t. fresh chives, minced

1 t. red pepper flakes
1 t. dried basil
1/4 t. garlic powder
1 lb. mozzarella cheese, cubed

In a large bowl, combine all ingredients except cheese; mix well. Add cheese cubes and stir to coat. Cover and refrigerate for one hour or overnight. Stir again to coat before serving. Serves 12.

Arrange grazing-board goodies like cured meats, cheese cubes, spiced nuts and dried fruits on a tiered cake stand. It looks so festive, and takes up less space on a buffet table.

Merry-Making
Appetizers

Marinated Mushrooms

Doreen Knapp
Stanfordville, NY

*These tasty mushrooms are great on a cheese board or as a little
"something extra" with any meal, including breakfast and lunch.
Sometimes I add hot red pepper flakes for a little spice.*

3/4 olive oil
1/3 c. red wine vinegar
1-1/2 t. salt
3/4 t. sugar
1/2 t. dried basil
6 whole peppercorns

1 clove garlic, pressed or minced
1 bay leaf
1-1/2 lbs. medium white
    mushrooms, trimmed
    and halved

In a saucepan, combine all ingredients except mushrooms. Bring to a
boil over medium-high heat; reduce heat to low. Cover and simmer
for 5 minutes. Stir in mushrooms. Simmer for 3 to 5 minutes, until
mushrooms are firm-tender but not mushy, stirring to coat mushrooms.
Transfer to a bowl; cover and refrigerate until cool. Discard bay leaf at
serving time. Makes 4 servings.

You've already trimmed the tree and beribboned the mantel...
just add a welcoming row of twinkling luminarias along
the front walk and your house will be party perfect!

Christmas
for Sharing

Marinated Brussels Sprouts

Julie Perkins
Anderson, IN

This recipe is how I got my family to eat Brussels sprouts! These are perfect for family gatherings...great at picnics with hamburgers and hot dogs too. If you prefer, use a pound of fresh small Brussels sprouts, trimmed and steamed until tender.

2 10-oz. pkgs. frozen Brussels
    sprouts
1/2 c. olive oil
1/2 c. tarragon vinegar
2 T. sugar
1 clove garlic, pressed

1 t. salt
1/2 t. seasoned salt
1 t. pepper
2 small onions, sliced and
    separated into rings

Cook Brussels sprouts according to package directions; drain. In a container with a lid, combine remaining ingredients except onions. Add sprouts and onions; place lid on container and shake well. Cover and refrigerate at least 24 hours before serving. Serves 6 to 8.

Smoked Pickled Eggs

Thomas Campbell
Brooklyn Park, MN

These eggs are simple and tasty treats I put out on the relish tray for the holidays. I make these ahead of time...the longer they are in the refrigerator, the more smoky flavor they have.

6 whole eggs
1-3/4 c. water
1/4 c. vinegar

2 t. smoke-flavored cooking
    sauce

Place eggs in a saucepan; cover with cool water. Bring to a boil over high heat. Turn off heat, leaving covered pan on stove. Let eggs stand in hot water until water is cool enough to handle eggs. Drain and peel eggs. Place warm eggs in a glass jar and set aside. In a bowl, combine water, vinegar and sauce; pour mixture over eggs. Cover and allow to cool to room temperature. Add jar lid; refrigerate until ready to serve. Serves 6; may slice eggs into halves or quarters for more servings.

Merry-Making
Appetizers

Cheesy Olives

Melanie Springer
Canton, OH

This is an old recipe that I used to make for get-togethers. I just made it again...I had forgotten how delicious it is! It's a great little finger food. These can be frozen up to a week on a sheet pan, unbaked and wrapped in aluminum foil. Unwrap; bake directly from the freezer for 20 to 25 minutes.

10-oz. jar green olives with
    pimentos, drained
1-1/2 c. shredded sharp
    Cheddar cheese

1 c. all-purpose flour
1/4 c. butter, softened
1/4 t. pepper
Optional: 1/4 t. smoked paprika

Pat olives dry; set aside. In a large bowl, mix remaining ingredients except olives in a bowl; knead mixture in bowl until dough forms. If too crumbly, add water, one teaspoon at a time, till dough forms. For each olive, pinch off small amount of dough. Flatten in your hand, wrap around an olive and roll in your hand until completely covered and smooth. Arrange olives on a baking sheet. Bake at 400 degrees for 15 to 20 minutes. Makes 6 to 8 servings.

A veggie topiary...clever! Simply use toothpicks to attach broccoli flowerets and cherry tomatoes to a styrofoam cone until the cone is completely covered. Garnish with cheese "ornaments" cut out with mini cookie cutters.

Christmas Wassail

Roberta Simpkins
Mentor on the Lake, OH

I got this family recipe from a friend, several years ago. We went over to visit and she had made this special hot beverage to warm us up! It has become a family favorite at all the holidays

64-oz. bottle apple juice
2 c. cranberry juice cocktail
3/4 c. sugar
1 t. allspice

2 4-inch cinnamon sticks
whole cloves to taste
1 whole orange

In a 3-quart slow cooker, combine juices, sugar, allspice and cinnamon sticks. Insert cloves in orange; add to crock. Cover and cook on low setting for 2 to 3 hours. Serve warm. Serves 10.

Spicy Apple Eggnog

Bethi Hendrickson
Danville, PA

This "adult" eggnog really hits the spot on a cold winter's night.

2 eggs, beaten
3 c. whole milk
2 c. light cream or fat-free
   half-and-half

1/3 c. sugar
1/2 t. cinnamon
3/4 c. apple brandy
Garnish: whipped cream, nutmeg

In a large saucepan, combine eggs, milk, cream or half-and-half, sugar and cinnamon. Cook and stir over medium heat until mixture is heated through and slightly thickened; do not boil. Remove from heat; stir in brandy. To serve, ladle one cup eggnog into a heat-proof glass or mug. Add a dollop of whipped cream and sprinkle with a little nutmeg. Makes 12 servings.

Make gift notes all year 'round...
in December, you'll know
just what to get everyone!

Merry-Making
Appetizers

Sassy Salsa

Laura Witham
Anchorage, AL

I love the taste of fresh salsa, especially the kind you get at authentic Mexican restaurants. So I decided to experiment and come up with my own. You won't believe how easy and how tasty this is!

28-oz. can whole peeled
    tomatoes, drained and rinsed
12-oz. can whole tomatillos,
    drained
1 white onion, cut into chunks

2 jalapeño peppers, or to taste
1 bunch fresh parsley or cilantro
2 t. garlic, minced
zest and juice of 1 lime
salt and pepper to taste

In a food processor, combine all ingredients except lime zest and juice, salt and pepper. Process until consistency is as thick or chunky as you like. Add lime zest and juice; season with salt and pepper and serve. Makes 8 servings.

Family favorites like homemade salsa, jams & jellies
are perfect hostess gifts...simply tie on a festive
bow and a gift tag!

Christmas
for Sharing

Hissy Fit Dip

*Laurie Wilson
Fort Wayne, IN*

*A wonderful dip with a funny name! Everyone wants
the recipe after they taste it at our get-togethers.*

1 lb. ground pork sausage
16-oz. container sour cream
8-oz. pkg. cream cheese,
  softened
1-1/2 t. Worcestershire sauce
1 t. dried parsley
1 t. onion powder
1/2 t. garlic powder

1/2 t. dried sage
8-oz. pkg. pasteurized process
  cheese, cubed
1 c. shredded Monterey Jack
  cheese
Optional: 2 T. fresh chives,
  minced
snack chips or baguette slices

Brown sausage in a skillet over medium heat; drain. Meanwhile,
combine sour cream and cream cheese in a large bowl; blend well.
Stir in Worcestershire sauce and seasonings until well mixed. Fold in
sausage, cheeses and chives, if using; mix thoroughly. Transfer mixture
to a lightly greased 9"x9" baking pan or 9" oven-safe skillet. Bake,
uncovered, at 350 degrees for 50 to 60 minutes, until bubbly, golden
and cheeses are melted. Serve hot with chips or baguette slices. Makes
6 to 8 servings.

Set out a bowl of unshelled walnuts or pecans and a nutcracker.
Guests will stay busy cracking nuts to snack on while
you put the finishing touches on dinner.

Merry-Making *Appetizers*

Donna's Sausage Dip

Donna Phair
Pittsfield, MA

Every Superbowl Sunday, I'm asked to make this dip. There is never any left by halftime! My nephew asked for the recipe...he likes to put it on his scrambled eggs! I've been making this dip since 2006 and it's my most-requested recipe at any gathering.

2 16-oz. pkgs. ground
   pork sausage
2 8-oz. pkgs. cream cheese,
   softened

2 14-1/2 oz. cans diced tomatoes
   with green chiles
tortilla chips or crackers

Brown sausage in a skillet over medium heat, chopping it as it cooks; drain. Add cream cheese and tomatoes with juice; reduce heat to low. Cover and cook until cream cheese is melted, stirring occasionally to blend ingredients. Transfer to a serving dish; serve hot with tortilla chips or crackers. Makes 20 servings.

Show off tiny ornaments on a mini table-top tree...
perfect for a buffet table.

Christmas
for Sharing

Cheeseburger Wontons

Tammy Rowe
Belleek, OH

All the cheeseburger flavors you like in a wonton cup! For a lower-calorie appetizer, rinse the browned beef well and use low-fat cheeses. Egg roll wrappers are usually found in the supermarket produce department.

1 lb. ground beef
1 onion, diced
8-oz. pkg. cream cheese,
    softened
1 T. catsup
1 T. mustard
1 t. onion powder

1 t. garlic powder
1 t. salt
1 t. pepper
24 large egg roll wrappers
1 c. shredded American or
    Cheddar cheese

Brown beef with onion in a skillet over medium heat; drain. Stir in cream cheese, catsup, mustard and seasonings. Cook over low heat until cream cheese is melted; stir well and set aside. Spray 12 muffin cups with non-stick vegetable spray; gently press one egg roll wrapper into each cup. Spray again; add another wrapper to each cup, facing the other direction. Spoon beef mixture equally into each cup; top with cheese. Bake at 350 degrees for 18 to 20 minutes. Serve hot. Makes one dozen.

Set out easy-to-handle foods and beverages at tables in several different rooms around the house. Guests will be able to snack and mingle easily.

Merry-Making
Appetizers

Layered Pizza Appetizer

JoAnn
Gooseberry Patch

*This yummy spread is so simple to make! It's quick to
whip up when friends are visiting.*

8-oz. pkg. cream cheese,
  softened
8-oz. container sour cream
1 t. pizza seasoning
3/4 c. pepperoni, chopped
1 c. lettuce, shredded

1/2 c. tomato, chopped
  and drained
2 T. sliced black olives, drained
3/4 c. shredded mozzarella
  cheese
baguette slices or tortilla chips

Combine cream cheese, sour cream and pizza seasoning in a large bowl.
Beat with an electric mixer on medium speed until smooth. Spoon
mixture onto a large serving plate; spread to within one inch of edge.
Top with pepperoni, lettuce, tomato and olives; sprinkle with mozzarella
cheese. Cover and chill until serving time. Serve with baguette slices or
tortilla chips. Makes 16 servings.

Delectable baked brie cheese with honey can be whipped up in
a jiffy. Cut the top off a small wheel of brie and place in a casserole
dish. Drizzle with 1/4 cup honey and bake at 350 degrees
for 5 to 7 minutes, until softened but not melting. Serve
with crisp crackers and a spreader.

Christmas
for Sharing

Wintry Warm Spiced Nuts

*Paula Marchesi
Auburn, PA*

This recipe is so perfect for the holidays, especially at Christmas, sitting around the fireplace, munching on these warm nuts. I often make a double batch, as they go fast. Make it your way...mix & match using your favorite nuts like cashews, walnuts or honey-roasted peanuts.

1 c. pecan halves	4-1/2 t. Worcestershire sauce
1 c. unblanched almonds	1 t. chili powder
1 c. unsalted dry-roasted peanuts	1/2 t. garlic salt
3 T. butter, melted	1/4 t. Cajun seasoning

Combine all nuts in a large bowl. Drizzle with melted butter and Worcestershire sauce; toss to coat. Spread mixture in a single layer on an ungreased 15"x10" jelly-roll pan. Bake at 300 degrees for 30 minutes, or until golden; remove from oven. Combine seasonings in a cup. Transfer warm nuts to a bowl; sprinkle with seasoning mixture and toss to coat well. Serve warm, or allow to cool before storing in an airtight container. Makes 3 cups.

Paper baking cups are available in many sizes and colors. They're an easy and festive way to serve individual snacks and desserts at holiday get-togethers.

Merry-Making
Appetizers

Candied Nuts

Peggy Borrok
Lafayette, LA

These tasty nuts are great alone or mixed into a homemade trail mix. They are also appreciated as a holiday gift. You can use one type of nut, or an assortment.

2-3/4 c. pecan halves, walnut
   halves and/or almonds
2 T. butter, divided
1 c. sugar

1/2 c. water
1/2 t. cinnamon
1/2 t. salt
1 t. vanilla extract

Spread nuts on an ungreased baking sheet. Bake at 250 degrees for 10 minutes; set aside. Meanwhile, use one tablespoon butter to coat a 15"x10" jelly-roll pan; set aside. Grease the sides of a heavy saucepan with remaining butter; add sugar, water, cinnamon and salt to saucepan. Cook and stir over medium-low heat until sugar dissolves, covering pan if needed. Increase heat to medium. Cook without stirring until mixture reaches the soft-ball stage, or 234 to 243 degrees on a candy thermometer. Remove from heat; add vanilla and nuts and stir. Spread onto prepared jelly-roll pan. Bake at 250 degrees for 30 minutes, stirring every 10 minutes. Spread nut mixture on wax paper to cool. Makes about 3 cups.

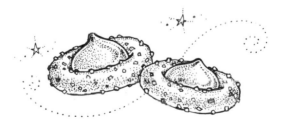

For easy bite-size treats, arrange round pretzels on a baking sheet; place a chocolate drop in the center of each. Bake at 350 degrees for one to 2 minutes, remove from oven and chill until set.

Christmas
for Sharing

French Onion Dip

Elisha Nelson
Brookline, MO

This quick & easy dip is great with chips and garden-fresh veggies!

16-oz. container sour cream
2 t. dried, minced onions
2 t. onion powder
1 t. garlic powder
1 t. dried parsley

1/2 t. turmeric
1/2 t. celery seed
1 t. sea salt
3/4 t. pepper

Mix together all ingredients in a bowl. Cover and refrigerate; chill for at least 2 hours before serving. Serves 6 to 8.

Curry Vegetable Dip

Lynnette Jones
East Flat Rock, NC

A family & friends favorite...serve with crisp veggies and crackers.

1 c. mayonnaise
1 t. prepared horseradish
1 t. white vinegar

1 t. onion, grated
1/2 t. curry powder

Combine all ingredients in a bowl. Mix well. Cover and chill at least one hour before serving. Makes 15 to 20 servings.

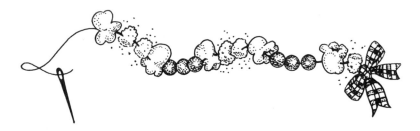

Enjoy some old-fashioned fun...stringing popcorn and cranberries. The kids will love it, and the strands are so pretty draped along a mantel, doorway and, of course, on the Christmas tree!

Merry-Making
Appetizers

Potato Chip Dip

Debbi Luckett
Mechanicsburg, OH

My mom used to make this dip for family get-togethers. Everyone always asked for the recipe. Serve with potato chips or corn chips.

16-oz. container sour cream
16-oz. jar mayonnaise
1 T. dried parsley
1 T. onion, minced
1 t. dried dill weed
3/4 t. Beau Monde seasoning

Mix all ingredients in a large bowl. Cover and refrigerate for several hours or overnight. Stir well before serving. Serves 10 to 12.

Chili Cheese Dip

Karen Fetcher
Griffin, IN

This recipe is terrific for get-togethers, holidays or even halve it just for the family. I use one can of chili with beans and one can without. We like a few beans, but not a lot...it's your choice!

1 lb. ground beef
3/4 c. onion, diced
2 4-oz. cans diced green chiles
2 15-oz. cans chili
16-oz. container pasteurized process cheese, cubed
tortilla chips

Cook beef and onion in a skillet over medium heat, crumbling beef finely; drain. Add remaining ingredients except chips; simmer until cheese is melted. If desired, transfer to a slow cooker; set on low for serving. Serve with tortilla chips. Makes 15 to 20 servings.

Make mini wreaths to slip around dinner napkins. Simply wind fresh rosemary stems into a ring shape, tuck in the ends and tie on a tiny bow...so festive!

Christmas
for Sharing

Black-Eyed Pea Dip

Kim Hinshaw
Cedar Park, TX

My husband's side of the family always ate black-eyed peas on New Year's Day for good luck. We needed a good way to get our children to eat them...this dip was the perfect way to disguise the little peas. It's great for game-day snacks.

16-oz. can black-eyed peas,
    drained and divided
3 green onions, chopped, green
    tops included
1/2 c. sour cream
1 t. granulated garlic

1/2 t. salt
1/2 c. chunky-style salsa
Optional: 4 slices bacon, crisply
    cooked and crumbled
corn chips

Reserving 1/3 cup peas, add peas to a blender or a food processor fitted with a steel blade. Process until smooth. Transfer to a bowl; blend in onions, sour cream, garlic and salt. Stir in reserved peas and salsa. Cover and refrigerate for 2 hours. At serving time, stir again; garnish with bacon, if desired. Serve with corn chips. Makes 2-1/2 cups.

Spiced Green Tea

Erin Brock
Charleston, WV

My guests enjoy this flavorful hot tea...it's a change from the usual holiday beverages! Float an orange slice in each cup, if you like.

4 c. boiling water
4 green tea bags
4 c. pineapple-orange juice
1 c. dried peaches, apricots
    and/or pears

6-inch stick cinnamon, broken
1 T. crystallized ginger, minced
Optional: sugar to taste

Combine boiling water and tea bags in a 4-quart slow cooker. Let stand for 5 minutes; discard tea bags. Add fruit juice, dried fruit and spices. Cover and cook on high setting for 2 to 3 hours. Strain, discarding fruit and spices. Ladle tea into cups. If desired, add sugar to taste. Makes 8 servings.

Merry-Making
Appetizers

Holiday Beef Cheese Ball

*Marlana Long
Waverly, OH*

This yummy cheese ball is always requested during the holidays for gatherings and parties. Some years, I have made a half-dozen of these cheese balls between Thanksgiving and Christmas...that's how much everyone likes them!

2 8-oz. pkgs. cream cheese,
  softened
2 to 3 2-oz. pkgs. sliced pressed
  beef, chopped

3 to 4 green onions, chopped
1 T. powdered flavor enhancer
1 T. Worcestershire sauce
snack crackers

Place cream cheese in a large bowl; set aside. Use a small food processor or a sharp knife to chop 2 packages beef and onions; add to cream cheese. Add flavor enhancer and Worcestershire sauce; blend well. Form into a ball and place on a serving plate. Use a spatula to smooth over the ball. If desired, a third package of chopped beef can be used to cover cheese ball. Cover and refrigerate for 2 hours. To serve, uncover; arrange crackers around cheese ball. Makes 8 to 10 servings.

Christmas is coming, the geese are getting fat,
Please to put a penny in an old man's hat.
If you haven't got a penny, then a ha'penny will do,
If you haven't got a ha'penny, then God bless you!
–Traditional English Carol

Christmas
for Sharing

Chipped Ham Sandwiches

Leona Krivda
Belle Vernon, PA

These sandwiches are really great to have on hand if you know you're having company, or for the kids after school. I got this recipe years ago from a friend.

1 c. butter, melted
3 T. mustard
2 T. onion, finely chopped
1-1/2 T. poppy seed

1 t. Worcestershire sauce
12 sandwich buns, split
1 lb. chipped deli baked ham
1 lb. sliced Swiss cheese

In a bowl, combine melted butter, mustard, onion, poppy seed and Worcestershire sauce. Spread mixture evenly on both cut sides of bun halves. Divide ham and cheese among bottom halves of buns, folding or cutting as needed; add bun tops. Place each sandwich on a square of aluminum foil; wrap up tight. Refrigerate up to 5 days, until ready to serve. To serve, take out as many sandwiches as needed; arrange on a baking sheet. Bake at 350 degrees for 20 minutes. Makes 12 sandwiches.

Host a holiday movie marathon! Toss pillows and quilts on the floor, set out plenty of snacks and have a non-stop viewing of all the best Christmas movies.

Merry-Making
Appetizers

Pizza Broiled Sandwiches

Marsha Baker
Pioneer, OH

My family has often enjoyed this easy recipe for parties and open houses...they've requested it as an easy meal so many times, too. The beef mixture keeps well in the fridge and you can make as many sandwiches at a time as you want.

1 lb. ground beef, browned
    and drained
16-oz. pkg. shredded Cheddar or
    Co-Jack cheese
1/2 c. onion, grated
6-oz. can chopped black olives,
    drained

10-3/4 oz. can tomato soup
1/3 c. oil
1/2 t. dried oregano
1 to 2 loaves French bread,
    halved lengthwise, or 12 to
    15 hamburger buns, split

In a large bowl, combine all ingredients except bread or buns; mix well. Cover and refrigerate for 4 hours. Spoon beef mixture onto cut sides of bread slices or buns, spreading all the way to the edges. Place on a broiler pan; broil for a few minutes, until browned. If using bread, slice on the diagonal for serving. Mixture keeps well in the refrigerator for a week. Makes 12 to 15 servings.

Dress up ruffled potato chips to serve with party sandwiches. Spread chips on a baking sheet and bake at 350 degrees for about 5 minutes, until warmed. Sprinkle with grated Parmesan cheese and Italian seasoning...yum!

Christmas
for Sharing

Wicked Shrimp Toasties

Lynda Hart
Bluffdale, UT

Everyone loves these delicious appetizers...they're great served warm. You may want to double the recipe!

24 slices very fresh sandwich
    bread, crusts trimmed
softened butter to taste
8-oz. pkg. cream cheese,
    softened
1/2 t. lemon juice

2 T. onion, finely diced
1/2 t. salt
1/4 t. Worcestershire sauce
6-oz. can tiny shrimp, drained
1 t. milk

Spread one side of each bread slice with butter; set aside. Combine remaining ingredients in a large bowl. Beat with an electric mixer on medium speed to a good spreading consistency, adding a little more milk if needed. Spread shrimp mixture on the unbuttered side of each bread slice. Roll up slices carefully, so the buttered side is exposed; arrange on a parchment paper-lined baking sheet. Broil until toasted on all sides, watching carefully to avoid burning. Serve warm. Makes 2 dozen.

Everything old is new again! A fondue pot is a must for keeping hot,
cheesy dips just right for serving. Simply fill the fondue pot,
turn it to the warm setting and forget about it.

Merry-Making
Appetizers

Baked Scotch Eggs

Julie Perkins
Anderson, IN

This is a great forgotten appetizer, a real family heirloom. Serve with a good mustard...your guests will be asking for your recipe!

1 doz. eggs, hard-boiled, peeled
2 lbs. ground pork sausage,
   room temperature
1/4 t. dried sage

2 eggs, beaten
16-oz. pkg. buttery round
   crackers, crushed
Garnish: mustard

Cover peeled eggs; keep warm. In a large bowl, combine sausage and sage; divide into 12 balls. Flatten into patties; hold each patty in your hand and wrap an egg, covering completely. Roll covered eggs in beaten egg, then into cracker crumbs. Place in an ungreased 13"x9" baking pan. Bake at 375 degrees for 30 minutes. Allow to cool. Cut eggs into quarters. Arrange on a platter and serve with mustard. Makes 4 dozen.

Christmas Eve Sausage Balls

Priscilla Howard
Morehead, KY

This is a great appetizer for Christmas Eve get-togethers. If there are any extras, they're good for a Christmas morning snack.

1 lb. spicy ground pork sausage
16-oz. pkg. shredded sharp
   Cheddar cheese

2 c. biscuit baking mix
1/4 c. milk
1 t. dried parsley

Combine all ingredients in a large bowl; mix well. Roll into small to medium-size balls and place on an oiled rimmed baking sheet, spacing one inch apart. Bake at 350 degrees for 20 to 25 minutes, until golden. Makes 2 to 2-1/2 dozen.

Cut out bite-size pieces of red and yellow peppers with a mini cookie cutter...what a clever way to trim a veggie dip platter!

Christmas
for Sharing

Apricot-Cranberry Relish

Vickie
Gooseberry Patch

Spoon this delectable relish over a block of cream cheese for an easy, tasty appetizer.

1 c. orange juice
1/2 c. plus 2 T. honey, divided
12-oz. pkg. fresh cranberries
1/2 c. dried apricots, finely
   chopped

1/4 c. crystallized ginger,
   finely chopped

Combine orange juice and 1/2 cup honey in a saucepan; bring to a boil. Add cranberries and bring to a boil; remove from heat. Drain; transfer to a bowl and let cool. Add remaining honey and other ingredients in a bowl; mix well and serve. Makes 3 cups.

Cranberry-Orange Spread

Lisa Smith
Huntington, IN

This yummy spread tastes just as good made with low-fat cream cheese. Serve with snowflake crackers, just for fun...and enjoy!

8-oz. pkg. cream cheese,
   softened
2 T. frozen orange juice
   concentrate
1 T. sugar

1/8 t. cinnamon
1/4 c. dried cranberries, chopped
1/4 c. pecans, finely chopped
zest of 1 orange
snack crackers

In a bowl, blend cream cheese, orange juice concentrate, sugar and cinnamon. Fold in remaining ingredients except crackers. Cover and refrigerate until serving time. Serve with crackers. Serves 4.

Nothing says Christmas like the scent of fresh-cut greenery! Stir up holiday sentiments by tucking balsam or pine sprigs between collectibles on a table or mantle.

Winter
Warming
Soups & Breads

Soup
Supper

Christmas
for Sharing

Grandma V's Veggie Beef Soup

Donna Viveiros
Fall River, MA

My family loves this soup, especially on a cold New England day after shoveling snow! This is a very versatile recipe. You can substitute ground turkey or pork for the ground beef, and if substituting, also use chicken broth in place of the beef broth. Any small soup pasta or rice may be used instead of the orzo, just increase your cooking time as needed.

1 lb. ground beef
1 T. butter
3/4 c. onion, diced
1 stalk celery, diced, leaves
    included if desired
1/2 t. salt
1/2 t. pepper
6 c. beef broth

1.35-oz. pkg. onion soup mix
14-1/2 oz. can petite diced
    tomatoes
16-oz. pkg. frozen mixed
    vegetables
2/3 c. orzo pasta, uncooked
Garnish: grated Parmesan cheese

In a large soup pot over medium heat, cook beef until no longer pink; drain and set aside in a bowl. To the same pot, add butter, onion, celery, salt and pepper; cook until onion is soft. Return beef to pot; add beef broth, soup mix, diced tomatoes with juice and vegetables. Bring to a boil; reduce heat to medium-low. Simmer for 15 minutes, stirring occasionally. Add pasta and cook for another 10 minutes, or until tender. Serve bowls of soup topped with Parmesan cheese. Serves 6 to 8.

Trimming the tree is such fun with friends. Put a big pot of soup on to simmer...when the last strand of tinsel is hung, dinner will be ready!

Winter Warming
Soups & Breads

Potato Soup Perfecto

Elle Roden
Houston, TX

This soup is so good on a cold winter's night...Grams loved it!
So full of good veggies.

6 russet potatoes, peeled and
   cut into 1/2-inch cubes
6 slices bacon, cut into
   1/2-inch pieces
3 T. butter
2 stalks celery, sliced
   1/4-inch thick
20 baby carrots, sliced
   1/4-inch thick
1/2 c. onion, diced

1 to 2 t. salt
1-1/2 t. pepper
3 T. all-purpose flour
1-1/2 c. chicken broth
2 c. half-and-half
dried thyme, cayenne pepper
   and nutmeg to taste
Garnish: finely sliced green
   onions, paprika

In a large saucepan, cover potatoes with water. Cook over medium-high heat until tender, 10 to 15 minutes. Drain and return to saucepan. Meanwhile, cook bacon in a skillet over medium heat until crisp. Drain; set aside bacon on paper towels. In same skillet, melt butter; add celery, carrots, onion, salt and pepper. Cook until vegetables are tender, about 10 minutes. Sprinkle with flour; cook and stir for 2 minutes. To potatoes in large saucepan, add chicken broth, half-and-half and seasonings to taste. Bring to a boil over high heat Stir in bacon; reduce heat to medium-low. Cook for 10 minutes, stirring occasionally. Ladle into soup bowls; garnish with sliced green onions and a sprinkle of paprika. Serves 4 to 6.

Winter is the time for comfort, for good food and warmth,
for the touch of a friendly hand and for a talk beside
the fire...it is the time for home.

–Dame Edith Sitwell

Christmas
for Sharing

Easy Chicken Noodle Soup

Jane Ivey
Winterville, GA

Easy but tastes homemade...much better than canned soup!

1/2 c. butter
2 c. carrots, peeled and grated
2 stalks celery, diced
1/2 c. onion, chopped
16-oz. pkg. angel hair pasta,
    divided and uncooked

2 32-oz. containers chicken
    broth
2 12-oz. cans white chicken,
    drained and flaked
garlic salt, salt and pepper
    to taste

Melt butter in a skillet over medium heat; sauté carrots, celery and onion until tender. Meanwhile, break half of pasta into thirds and cook according to package directions; reserve remaining pasta for another recipe. Drain pasta; return to pan. Add vegetable mixture, chicken broth, chicken and seasonings. Simmer over low heat for about one hour, stirring occasionally. Makes 8 to 10 servings.

Simple Tomato-Rice Soup

Wendy Jacobs
Idaho Falls, ID

My family loves to warm up with mugs of hot soup after
an afternoon of sledding. This soup is ready in a jiffy!

1/4 c. onion, diced
1/4 c. green pepper, diced
1 to 2 t. olive oil
10-3/4 oz. can tomato soup

1-1/4 c. water
3/4 to 1 c. instant rice, uncooked
1 t. Italian seasoning, or to taste

In a skillet over medium heat, sauté onion and green pepper in oil for about 4 to 5 minutes, until tender. Meanwhile, whisk together soup and water in a saucepan; heat through over medium heat. Add onion mixture, rice and seasoning. Simmer over medium-low heat for 10 minutes, or until rice is tender. Serves 2 to 3.

Set a teeny-tiny snowman at each person's place...so cute! Simply glue white pompoms together with craft glue, then add faces and scarves clipped from bits of felt.

Winter Warming
Soups & Breads

Cream of Chicken Soup

Carla McRorie
Kannapolis, NC

I've always loved this made-from-scratch soup and have tweaked it through the years. There's nothing like good soup on a cold day! For a variation, omit the milk and flour. Cook 2 cups rice or fine egg noodles until half done; add to broth and simmer until tender. Serve with cornbread or crackers.

3-lb. whole chicken	1 c. milk
salt and pepper to taste	2 T. all-purpose flour
3 T. butter	3 to 4 T. cold water

In a soup pot, cover chicken with water; season with salt and pepper. Simmer for 45 minutes to one hour, until chicken is very tender. Remove chicken to a plate; set aside to cool, reserving broth in pan. Add butter and additional salt and pepper as needed to reserved broth. Bring broth to a boil; stir in milk. In a cup, combine flour and enough water to make a thin paste. Stir into hot broth; cook and stir until thickened as desired. Shred or cube chicken and add to soup; heat through and serve. Makes 6 servings.

Buttermilk Biscuit Pan Bread

Teresa Verell
Roanoke, VA

This simple recipe has been a family favorite for over 20 years.

3 c. self-rising flour	1/2 c. oil
2 c. buttermilk	

In a large bowl, stir together all ingredients. Pour batter into a greased 13"x9" baking pan. Smooth out batter in pan. Bake at 450 degrees for 10 to 12 minutes. Cut into squares. Makes one dozen.

Freeze wrappers from sticks of butter in a plastic zipping bag.... handy whenever you need to grease a baking pan!

Christmas
for Sharing

Slow-Cooker Pepper Jack
White Chicken Chili

Sherry Sheehan
Evensville, TN

I have created some of my best recipes by modifying ingredients from a couple of other recipes and adding other items from my pantry. This tasty slow-cooker chili is one of those.

2-1/2 lbs. chicken tenderloins
2 15-1/2 oz. cans cannellini
   beans, drained
28-oz. can green enchilada sauce
3 c. low-sodium chicken broth
1 c. onion, diced
10-oz. can diced tomatoes with
   green chiles
8-oz. pkg. shredded Pepper
   Jack cheese

1 c. whipping cream
1/2 c. cream cheese, softened
1/2 c. regular or jalapeño
   salsa verde
1/2 t. salt
1/4 t. white pepper
Garnish: salsa verde-flavored
   tortilla chips

Line a 6-quart slow cooker with a disposable liner. Add chicken, beans, enchilada sauce, chicken broth and onion to slow cooker. Cover and cook on low setting for 6 to 7-1/2 hours. Remove chicken to a bowl; shred chicken and return to slow cooker. Add tomatoes with juice and remaining ingredients except garnish. Cook an additional 30 minutes, or until cheeses are melted; stir well. Serve in bowls, with tortilla chips as a topping or on the side. Makes 6 to 8 servings.

Celebrate Christmas Texas-style! Set out cowboy boots
in front of the fireplace instead of hanging stockings.

Winter Warming
Soups & Breads

Slow-Cooker Creamy Chicken Enchilada Soup

Rachel Kowasic
Valrico, FL

This was a "use what's in the fridge and pantry" kind of recipe. It came out so delicious, I have to share! Wonderful served with your favorite toppings.

4 to 5 boneless, skinless
   chicken breasts
15-1/2 oz. can black beans
10-3/4 oz. can Cheddar cheese
   soup
10-oz. can red enchilada sauce
4-oz. can diced green chiles

1 c. frozen corn
1 c. chicken broth
1 T. dried cilantro
Garnish: shredded cheese, sour
   cream, chopped tomatoes,
   avocado and green onions,
   tortilla chips

Combine all ingredients except garnish in a 5-quart slow cooker; mix gently. Cover and cook on low setting for 6 to 8 hours, until chicken is very tender. Remove chicken and shred; stir into soup. Garnish as desired. Makes 6 servings.

Fresh-baked bread bowls...simple! Thaw one to 2 loaves frozen bread dough according to package directions. Cut each loaf into 3 pieces; shape into balls and place on large sprayed baking sheets. Cover with sprayed plastic wrap; let rise until double in size. Uncover and bake at 350 degrees for 25 minutes, or until golden. Cut off tops, hollow out and fill with soup.

Christmas
for Sharing

Mom's Slow-Cooker Lasagna Soup *Jackie Selover*
Sidney, OH

I love to put this soup into the slow cooker in the morning before work, and come home to find the house smelling so good! I just add a tossed salad and garlic bread, and we have a great satisfying meal, with leftovers for lunch the next day.

1 lb. Italian ground pork sausage
    or hot breakfast sausage
1 T. olive oil
2 green peppers, chopped
1/4 c. onion, chopped
2 cloves garlic, minced
28-oz. can whole peeled
    tomatoes, chopped
6-oz. can tomato paste

6 c. chicken broth
1 t. Italian seasoning
1 t. sugar
salt and pepper to taste
8 lasagna noodles, uncooked
    and broken
Garnish: shredded Parmesan
    or mozzarella cheese, or
    ricotta cheese

In a skillet over medium heat, brown sausage in oil; drain. Transfer to a 5-quart slow cooker. Add remaining ingredients except garnish. Cover and cook on low setting for 4 to 5 hours, until bubbly and pasta is tender. Garnish as desired. Makes 6 servings.

Slow cookers are so convenient...why not put one on your
Christmas wish list? A 4 to 6-quart slow cooker is ideal
for family-size recipes and roasts, while a 2-1/2 quart size
is just right for sides and appetizers.

Winter Warming
Soups & Breads

Parmesan-Garlic Monkey Bread

Linda Diepholz
Lakeville, MN

This is a tasty bread to serve with lasagna,
spaghetti or just about anything Italian.

2 T. butter, melted
2 T. grated Parmesan cheese
1/2 t. garlic powder
1 t. Italian seasoning
12-oz. tube refrigerated biscuits,
    quartered

1/2 c. shredded Italian 5-cheese
    blend or mozzarella cheese
Garnish: warmed spaghetti or
    pizza sauce

Mix butter, Parmesan cheese and seasonings in a large bowl until
blended. Add biscuit pieces; toss to coat. Arrange biscuit pieces in a
9" round cake pan sprayed with non-stick vegetable spray. Top with
shredded cheese. Bake at 350 degrees for 20 to 25 minutes, until
golden. Let cool in pan for 10 minutes; turn out onto a wire rack and
cool slightly. Serve with warmed sauce. Serves 10.

Jam jars filled with old-fashioned hard candies make fun gifts...
great as table decorations and party favors, too! Cover jar lids
with a circle of fabric, cut with pinking shears and tied
on with a pretty ribbon.

Christmas
for Sharing

Slow-Cooker Creamy Wild Rice Soup

Donna Wilson
Maryville, TN

This soup tastes so good on a cold winter's day. It just simmers in the slow cooker all day while we're out enjoying sunny weather.

1 lb. ground beef, browned
   and drained
6-oz. pkg. long-grain and wild
   rice soup mix, cooked
1 small butternut squash, peeled
   and cubed
1 red onion, chopped
1 carrot, peeled and shredded
1 c. fresh kale, chopped

1 clove garlic, minced
10-3/4 oz. can cream of
   mushroom soup
1-1/2 c. milk
1 c. chicken broth
1 c. shredded Cheddar cheese
1-oz. pkg. ranch salad
   dressing mix
Optional 1/2 c. dried cranberries

Combine all ingredients in a 6-quart slow cooker; stir. Cover and cook on low setting for 4 to 6 hours. Stir again before serving. Makes 12 servings.

Tote along thermoses filled with hot soup on a visit to the Christmas tree farm...it'll really hit the spot!

Winter Warming
Soups & Breads

Roasted Butternut Squash Soup *Bethi Hendrickson*
Danville, PA

*I love adding my cinnamon-toasted pumpkin seeds to a bowl
of this yummy harvest soup. This is a recipe where you
can definitely put that hand stick blender to good use.*

2 butternut squash, halved and
    seeds removed
8 slices bacon
3 T. olive oil, divided
3 T. butter

1/4 c. onion, chopped finely
1 t. ground ginger
3 c. chicken broth
2 T. brown sugar, packed
Garnish: sour cream

Arrange squash halves cut-side down on a parchment paper-lined
rimmed baking sheet, placing 2 slices bacon under each half. Rub
squash skins with a little olive oil. Bake at 350 degrees for 45 minutes,
or until fork-tender. Set aside squash to cool; peel and dice squash.
Meanwhile, in a stockpot or Dutch oven over medium heat, melt butter
with remaining oil. Add onion and cook for 3 to 4 minutes, until tender.
Add ginger; cook for one more minute. Add chicken broth and brown
sugar; mix well. Add diced squash. Cover and simmer for 5 to
8 minutes, until squash is very tender. Purée mixture in pan with
an immersion blender, or in small batches in a regular blender. Simmer
for 2 minutes, or until heated through. Garnish with sour cream and
Cinnamon-Toasted Pumpkin Seeds, as desired. Serves 6 to 8.

Cinnamon-Toasted Pumpkin Seeds:

1/2 c. pumpkin seeds, rinsed
1 egg white, beaten

cinnamon to taste

Place pumpkin seeds in a bowl; add just enough egg white to make
seeds tacky. Add cinnamon; mix well. Spread on a parchment paper-
lined baking sheet. Bake at 350 degrees for 3 minutes; mix well.
Continue baking, checking every minute, until toasted as desired.

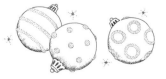

Christmas
for Sharing

Sausage & Lentil Soup

Elizabeth Cerri
Stephens City, VA

*Over the years, I have modified this soup from pork sausage
to turkey sausage. To my surprise, you can get this
same soup at a favorite Italian restaurant.*

3 T. olive oil
3/4 c. onion, diced
3 cloves garlic, diced
1 green, red or yellow
   pepper, diced
1 stalk celery, diced
1 carrot, peeled and diced
4 hot Italian turkey sausage
   links, casings removed and
   broken up
14-1/2 oz. can diced tomatoes

1 T. red pepper flakes, or to taste
1 t. dried oregano
1 t. dried thyme
1 t. dried parsley
1 t. dried basil
32-oz. container chicken or
   vegetable broth
1 c. dried brown lentils, rinsed
   and sorted
salt and pepper to taste

Heat oil in a stockpot over medium-high heat; add diced vegetables.
Cook until onion is translucent and vegetables start to soften. Reduce
heat to medium. Add sausage to vegetable mixture. Cook until sausage
is no longer pink, but not cooked all the way through. Stir in tomatoes
with juice, red pepper flakes and herbs; simmer for 3 to 5 minutes.
Stir in broth and lentils. Cover and simmer over low heat for about
30 minutes, stirring occasionally, until vegetables and lentils are tender.
Season with salt and pepper. Serves 8 to 10.

Candy cane-style napkin rings are so simple to make. Twist
together red and white pipe cleaners and slip napkins inside.

Winter Warming
Soups & Breads

Herbed Peasant Bread

Denise Webb
Bloomingdale, GA

I've had this recipe for so many years and it is always welcomed during the cold winter months. It is especially good with a hot, steamy bowl of soup.

1/2 c. onion, chopped
3 T. butter
1 c. plus 2 T. very warm milk,
    about 120 to 130 degrees
1 T. sugar
1-1/2 t. salt

1/2 t. dried dill weed
1/2 t. dried rosemary
1/2 t. dried basil
1 env. active dry yeast
3 to 3-1/2 c. all-purpose flour
Garnish: melted butter

In a skillet over medium-low heat, sauté onion in butter until tender. Cool for 10 minutes; transfer to a large bowl. Add warm milk, sugar, salt, herbs, yeast and 3 cups flour; beat until smooth. Add enough of remaining flour to form a soft dough. Turn out onto a floured surface; knead until smooth and elastic, about 6 to 8 minutes. Place dough in a greased bowl, turning once to grease top. Cover with a tea towel and let rise in a warm place until doubled, about 45 minutes. Punch down dough; shape into a ball and place on a greased baking sheet. Cover and let rise until doubled, about 45 minutes. Bake at 375 degrees for 25 to 30 minutes. Remove to a wire rack; brush with melted butter. Cool and slice. Makes one loaf.

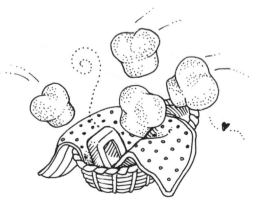

Slip a terra-cotta warming tile into a napkin-lined basket of freshly baked bread to keep it warm and tasty all through dinner.

95

Christmas
for Sharing

Old-World Beefy Onion Soup
Wendy Lee Paffenroth
Pine Island, NY

This soup is wonderful...just like you get in restaurants. It's always better the next day. I live in a farming area where acres & acres of onions are raised. Over many years of marriage, I've developed lots of great onion recipes.

6 to 8 c. chicken broth
1 to 1-1/2 lbs. beef chuck steak
   or London broil
1/4 c. butter
6 to 8 Pine Island onions, sliced
1/4 c. sugar
2 T. plus 1 t. all-purpose flour

1 c. white wine, cream sherry or
   chicken broth
salt and pepper to taste
6 to 8 slices French bread,
   toasted
Optional: shredded Parmesan or
   sliced mozzarella cheese

In a large stockpot, combine chicken broth and beef; bring to a boil. Simmer until beef is falling-apart tender, adding some water if broth cooks down too much. Remove beef to a plate, reserving broth; cool and dice beef, discarding any fat. Return beef to broth in stockpot. Meanwhile, melt butter in a large skillet. Add onions; cook until translucent. Stir in sugar; continue cooking. Sprinkle with flour; cook until starting to thicken. Stir in wine, sherry or broth. Simmer until most of the liquid is gone, stirring occasionally. Add onion mixture to beef mixture; simmer over low heat for about 2 hours. Season with a little salt and pepper. For best flavor, cool and refrigerate overnight. To serve, reheat soup; ladle soup into 6 to 8 oven-proof crocks or soup bowls. Top each with a slice of bread and a little cheese, if desired. Set crocks on a baking sheet. Bake at 325 degrees for a few minutes, until cheese is melted. Serves 6 to 8.

Baby photos make the sweetest placecards...just copy,
cut out and place in mini frames.

Winter Warming
Soups & Breads

Creamy Cauliflower Soup

Miriam Ankerbrand
Greencastle, PA

One evening, I wanted to make mashed cauliflower. But, I forgot that I had already added the cream and it got a little soupy...that got me thinking it would make a great soup. I looked up some other cream soup recipes I had and came up with this comforting soup.

1/2 c. onion diced
2 stalks celery, finely chopped
2 T. butter
1 head cauliflower, diced
6 c. chicken broth

salt and pepper to taste
1/2 c. whipping cream
Optional: 2 T. fresh parsley,
   finely chopped

In a large saucepan over medium heat, sauté onion and celery in butter until tender. Add cauliflower, chicken broth, salt and pepper; bring to a boil. Reduce heat to low; cover and simmer until cauliflower is very tender, about 20 to 25 minutes. Purée mixture in pan with an immersion blender, or in small batches in a regular blender, until completely smooth and thick. Add cream; mix well and heat through. Season with more salt and pepper if needed. Stir in parsley, if desired, and serve. Makes 6 servings.

Pass along Grandma's soup tureen to a new bride...
fill it with favorite seasonings and tie on
a cherished soup recipe.

Christmas
for Sharing

Yummy Chicken Broccoli-Wild Rice Soup

Denise Webb
Bloomingdale, GA

When I had some leftover long-grain & wild rice, I decided to toss together a soup using the leftovers. So I added some chicken broth, chicken, broccoli and cream cheese. It made a delicious soup! Now, I don't wait for leftovers, but make the whole mix into a great soup that we all enjoy. All my friends have asked for the recipe after tasting this yummy soup.

6-oz. pkg. long-grain and
    wild rice mix
12-oz. pkg frozen chopped
    broccoli
1/2 c. onion, chopped
1/2 c. celery, chopped
1/2 c. carrots, peeled and
    chopped

2 c. cooked chicken, cubed or
    shredded
4 c. chicken broth, or more
    as desired
8-oz. pkg. cream cheese,
    cubed

In a large saucepan, prepare rice mix as directed on package. Separately cook broccoli according to package directions, just until tender. Meanwhile, in a skillet over medium heat, sauté onion, celery and carrot in olive oil. Add vegetable mixture, broccoli and chicken to cooked rice. Stir in chicken broth to desired consistency; bring to a boil. Simmer for about 10 to 15 minutes. Stir in cream cheese; simmer until cream cheese is melted and well blended. Makes 4 to 6 servings.

For a welcoming scent of Christmas, fill a vintage teakettle with water, then add mulling spices and cinnamon sticks. Let it gently simmer on the stove so the sweet fragrance fills your home.

Winter Warming
Soups & Breads

Buttery Crescent Rolls

Kathleen Sturm
Corona, CA

Using a bread machine to make the dough for these scrumptious rolls makes it so easy! They are great to freeze and pull out for a nice addition to a quick weeknight meal...perfect for a special holiday meal too. These can also be frozen before baking. Just shape and freeze the crescents before second rise and baking; allow to thaw and rise, then bake as usual.

1/2 c. warm milk, about 110 to
   115 degrees
1/2 c. warm water, about 110 to
   115 degrees
1/2 c. butter, softened

1 egg, lightly beaten
4 c. bread flour
1/3 c. sugar
3/4 t. salt
1 T. instant dry yeast

Add all ingredients to a bread machine in the order listed, or according to your machine's directions for dough. Choose the "dough" cycle. When dough cycle is complete, divide dough into 2 equal balls. On a floured surface, roll out one ball into a 12-inch circle. Using a pizza cutter, cut circle into 12 wedges. Roll up each wedge to make a crescent shape, starting with the wide end. Place formed crescents seam-side down, on a greased baking sheet, leaving enough space to allow for rising. Repeat with remaining dough. Cover and let stand in a warm spot until rolls double in size, about 45 minutes. Uncover and bake at 350 degrees for about 15 to 20 minutes, until golden. Makes 2 dozen.

A tiered cake stand is just right for holding a variety of breads
to serve with dinner. Fill the tiers with savory garlic knots,
slices of marble rye, crescent rolls and bread sticks.

Christmas
for Sharing

Chicken Meatballs & Stars Soup

Diana Chaney
Olathe, KS

My kids love a bowl of this yummy soup after coming in from sledding and building snowmen. Sometimes I make it with alphabet noodles, just for fun.

1 lb. ground chicken
1 egg, beaten
1/2 c. panko bread crumbs
1/4 c. grated Parmesan cheese
1/4 c. fresh chives, finely
   chopped
1/2 t. garlic powder
3/4 t. salt

1/8 t. pepper
2 T. olive oil, divided
2 carrots, peeled and sliced
1/2 c, onion, chopped
6 c. low-sodium chicken broth
1 c. star-shaped small pasta,
   uncooked
salt and pepper to taste

In a large bowl, combine chicken, egg, bread crumbs, cheese, chives and seasonings. Mix well and form into small balls; arrange on a parchment paper-lined rimmed baking sheet. Drizzle with one tablespoon olive oil. Bake at 375 degrees for about 20 minutes, until golden and no longer pink inside. Meanwhile, heat remaining oil in a large soup pot over medium heat. Add carrots and onion; cook until softened. Add chicken broth and bring to a boil. Stir in pasta; cook for 4 to 6 minutes, until almost tender. Season with additional salt and pepper; stir in meatballs. Ladle into bowls and serve. Serves 6.

If the kids are getting cabin fever on a snowy day, send 'em outdoors with bottles of colored water to squirt holiday messages on the freshly fallen snow.

Winter Warming
Soups & Breads

Holiday Orange Bread

Judith Smith
Bellevue, WA

I received this recipe in the 1960s from my aunt, who is no longer living. We enjoyed this delicious bread during the holidays for many years.

3 c. all-purpose flour
4-1/2 t. baking powder
1/4 t. salt
1/3 c. butter

1 c. sugar
1 egg, lightly beaten
1/3 c. orange zest
1 c. orange juice

In a large bowl, combine flour, baking powder and salt; set aside. In a separate bowl, beat butter until soft. Gradually add sugar and continue beating until light and fluffy. Add egg and beat well. Add orange zest and juice; mix well. Add butter mixture to flour mixture; stir until moistened. Turn batter into a greased 9"x5" loaf pan. Bake at 350 degrees for one hour. Turn loaf out of pan onto a wire rack. Slice when cooled. Makes one loaf.

Combine an 8-ounce package of softened cream cheese with 1/4 cup apricot preserves; stir until smooth. So delicious on warm slices of quick bread!

Christmas
for Sharing

Slow-Cooker Sausage & Vegetable Soup

Ann Benfield
Port Charlotte, FL

This soup is excellent for winter...the flavor is wonderful! It uses eleven different vegetables, but feel free to mix & match what your family likes, or whatever you have on hand. You can add your favorite herbs, too.

1 lb. ground pork sausage
10-3/4 oz. can cream of
   mushroom soup
10-3/4 oz. can Cheddar
   cheese soup
4 c. water
14-1/2 oz. can stewed tomatoes
5 cubes chicken bouillon
1 small butternut squash, peeled
   and chopped
4 c. cabbage, chopped
5 redskin potatoes, peeled
   and cubed

1 turnip, peeled and chopped
1 onion, chopped
1 zucchini, chopped
1 yellow squash, chopped
4 stalks celery, chopped
3 carrots, peeled and thinly sliced
1/2 lb. green beans, trimmed
2 to 3 t. Worcestershire sauce
1 T. dried parsley
3/4 t. pepper
12-oz. can evaporated milk

Brown sausage in a large skillet over medium heat. Drain; transfer to a 6-quart slow cooker. Stir in soups and water until well blended. Add tomatoes with juice and remaining ingredients except milk; stir well. Cover and cook on low setting for 9 to 10 hours, until vegetables are tender. Stir in milk; cover and cook 30 minutes longer.

My idea of Christmas, whether old-fashioned or modern,
is very simple: loving others. Come to think of it,
why do we have to wait for Christmas to do that?

–Bob Hope

Winter Warming
Soups & Breads

7-Can Soup

Teri Gailey
Bryan, TX

I serve this soup with cornbread, but it's great on its own
and enjoyed as leftovers too. Yummy!

15-1/2 oz. can kidney beans
15-1/2 can pinto beans
15-1/2 can black beans
15-oz. can chili, no beans
15-oz. can corn
14-1/2 oz. can diced tomatoes

10-oz. can diced tomatoes with
   green chiles
salt and pepper to taste
8-oz. pkg. shredded Cheddar
   cheese

Add contents of all cans to a large soup pot; do not drain. Bring to a boil over medium-high heat, stirring occasionally. Reduce heat to medium-low and simmer for 10 to 15 minutes. Season with salt and pepper. Add cheese; stir until melted. Serve immediately. Makes 6 servings.

Lisa's Honey Cornbread

Lisa Green
Parkersburg, WV

I make this cornbread for my husband...he loves it!

1 c. all-purpose flour
1 c. yellow cornmeal
1/4 c. sugar
1 T. baking powder
1/2 t. salt

2 eggs, room temperature
1 c. whipping cream
1/4 c. canola oil
1/4 c. honey

In a bowl, combine flour, cornmeal, sugar, baking powder and salt; set aside. Beat eggs in a small bowl. Add cream, oil and honey; beat well. Stir egg mixture into flour mixture, just until moistened. Pour batter into a greased 9"x9" baking pan. Bake at 400 degrees for 20 to 25 minutes, until a toothpick inserted in the center comes out clean. Cut into squares; serve warm. Makes 9 servings.

Christmas
for Sharing

Slow-Cooker Broccoli-Cheese Soup

Krista Marshall
Fort Wayne, IN

Nothing tastes better than a big bowl of a favorite soup after a long day! Cold Indiana days mean we eat soup often during the winter months. We love broccoli-cheese soup, and this version uses fresh broccoli for the best flavor. Plus, the slow cooker helps me on extra busy days!

5 c. broccoli, finely chopped
2 stalks celery, diced
1 c. yellow onion, diced
2 T. butter
1/2 t. garlic powder
salt and pepper to taste

1/4 c. cornstarch
5 c. chicken broth
1-1/2 c. whipping cream
16-oz. pkg, shredded Cheddar
cheese
Optional: additional cheese

Add broccoli, celery, onion and butter to a 5-quart slow cooker. Season with garlic powder, salt and pepper; set aside. In a bowl, whisk together cornstarch and chicken broth; add to slow cooker and stir well. Cover and cook on low setting for 4 to 6 hours. Add cream and stir well. Add cheese in batches, stirring between each. Cover and cook on high setting for 30 minutes, or until cheese is melted and well blended. Garnish servings with extra cheese, if desired. Makes 6 to 8 servings.

A basket filled with warm and cozy blankets sitting alongside
a stack of favorite holiday stories will invite little ones
to snuggle in for bedtime stories.

Winter Warming
Soups & Breads

Creamy Potato Soup

Mary Little
Franklin, TN

This is an easy recipe that can be fixed quickly and enjoyed on a cold, snowy day.

2 to 3 T. butter
1 c. onion, chopped
2 to 3 stalks celery, chopped
3 to 4 c. potatoes, peeled
   and diced

2 c. water
2 10-3/4 oz. cans cream of
   chicken soup
2-1/2 c. milk
1 t. salt

Melt butter in a stockpot over medium heat. Add onion and celery; cook until tender and lightly golden. Add potatoes and water. Cover and simmer for about 15 minutes, until potatoes are tender. Whisk in chicken soup, milk and salt; heat through, but don't boil. Makes 8 servings.

Slow-Cooker Steakhouse Mushroom Soup

Emily Machula
Waukegan, IL

My favorite order at our local steakhouse is the London broil. This soup combines all those flavors into one comforting bowl.

15-oz. can diced potatoes,
   drained
1 lb. lean ground beef
10-oz. pkg. frozen chopped
   onions
10-oz. pkg. sliced mushrooms
1 T. oil

2 10-3/4 oz. cans golden
   mushroom soup
2 c. sodium-free beef broth
1 t. red steak sauce or
   Worcestershire sauce
Optional: 1/2 to 1 c. water

Add potatoes to a 5-quart slow cooker; set aside. Brown beef in a skillet over medium heat; drain and add to slow cooker. In same skillet, sauté onions and mushrooms in oil; drain and add to slow cooker. In a bowl, whisk together mushroom soup, beef broth and sauce; spoon over beef mixture. If desired, stir in additional water to desired consistency. Cover and cook on high setting for 4 hours. Serves 4 to 6.

Christmas
for Sharing

Slow-Cooker Ham Bone Soup

Cheryl Culver
Coyle, OK

Don't toss out that ham bone after the holidays...save it,
even freeze it until you're ready for this creamy soup.
It's so good and uses all your ham.

1 meaty ham bone
Optional: 1 lb. smoked pork
    sausage, sliced
32-oz. container chicken broth
6 redskin potatoes, cubed
4 carrots, peeled and chopped
2 stalks celery, chopped

1 onion, chopped
1 c. frozen corn
1 T. fresh parsley, chopped
1 to 2 t. garlic, minced
1 c. milk
salt and pepper to taste

In a 5-quart slow cooker, combine all ingredients except milk, salt and pepper. Cover and cook on low setting for 6 to 8 hours. Remove ham bone from slow cooker and cool; pull meat off bone and shred. Return meat to slow cooker and discard ham bone. With an immersion blender, slightly beat to thicken, adding enough milk for a creamy consistency. Season with salt and pepper and serve. Makes 6 to 8 servings.

Don't forget the family dog! Tie dog bones and small toys to
a greenery wreath using raffia...the perfect pooch present!

Winter Warming
Soups & Breads

Refrigerator Rolls

Michele Shenk
Manheim, PA

When I was learning to make homemade rolls, this recipe was a success. My family just loves to eat them and can't stop! It's a great recipe to use when doing a lot of cooking, as you can mix the dough the evening before and let it rise overnight in the refrigerator.

1 env. active dry yeast
2-1/2 c. warm water, about
   110-115 degrees, divided
1/2 c. shortening

1/2 c. sugar
1 egg, beaten
1-1/2 t. salt
7 c. all-purpose flour, divided

In a small bowl, dissolve yeast in 1/2 cup of warm water; set aside. In a large bowl, blend shortening and sugar. Add egg, salt, yeast mixture, remaining warm water and 4 cups flour. Beat until smooth; add enough of remaining flour to form a soft dough. Turn dough out onto a floured surface and knead until smooth and elastic, about 6 to 8 minutes. Place dough in a greased bowl, turning once to grease top. Cover and refrigerate for 8 hours, or overnight. Punch dough down and divide into 3 portions. Shape each portion into 12 rolls. Place rolls on greased baking sheets. Cover and let rise in a warm place for about one hour, until doubled. Bake at 350 degrees for 15 to 18 minutes, until golden. Makes 3 dozen.

Give homemade bread a beautiful finish...it's so easy! Whisk together a tablespoon of water with an egg yolk for a golden finish, or an egg white for a shiny luster. Brush over bread just before baking.

Christmas
for Sharing

Beef Taco Soup

Gladys Kielar
Whitehouse, OH

*At our house, soup season is all year 'round. Top this soup
with cheese, sour cream and tortilla chips...yum!*

2 lbs. lean ground beef
1 c. onion, chopped
2 1-1/4 oz. pkgs. mild taco
   seasoning mix
2 1-oz. pkgs. ranch salad
   dressing mix
3 14-1/2 oz. cans chicken broth,
   divided

28-oz. can crushed tomatoes
15-oz. can chili hot beans
15-oz. can corn, drained
1 t. sugar
Garnish: shredded Cheddar
   cheese, sour cream, crushed
   tortilla chips

In a large skillet over medium heat, cook beef with onion until beef is
browned and onion is clear. Drain; stir in seasoning mixes. Add one can
chicken broth to skillet; heat through and set aside. In a large soup pot,
combine remaining cans of broth and undrained tomatoes; bring to a
boil. Add beef mixture, undrained beans, corn and sugar; stir well.
Return to a boil; reduce heat to medium-low. Cover and simmer for
20 minutes. Serve with desired toppings. Makes 8 servings.

Crunchy tortilla strips are a crunchy addition to southwestern-style
soups. Cut corn tortillas into thin strips, then deep-fry quickly.
Drain on paper towels before sprinkling over bowls of soup.
Add some avocado wedges too...delicious!

Winter Warming
Soups & Breads

Chicken Tortilla Soup

Sheila Murray
Tehachapi, CA

*I love to make this hearty, super-easy soup when it's
cold outside. It really warms the soul!*

4 boneless, skinless chicken
   breasts
2 14-1/2 oz. cans Mexican
   stewed tomatoes or diced
   tomatoes with green chiles
2 15-1/2 oz. cans black beans

15-oz. can tomato sauce
4-oz. can diced green chiles
1 c. favorite salsa
Garnish: tortilla chips, shredded
   Cheddar cheese

Combine all ingredients except garnish in a 6-quart slow cooker; do
not drain tomatoes and beans. Cover and cook on low setting for 7 to
8 hours, until chicken is tender. Just before serving, remove chicken
to a plate; cut into bite-sized cubes. Stir chicken into soup. To serve,
add a handful of chips to each soup bowl. Ladle soup over chips; top
with cheese. Makes 6 to 8 servings.

Sour Cream Corn Muffins

Dale Duncan
Waterloo, IA

*Whenever I serve soup or chili, a basket of these delicious muffins
is on the table. Sometimes I'll sprinkle some fresh corn kernels
into the batter. Yum!*

1 c. yellow cornmeal
1 c. all-purpose flour
1/4 c. sugar
2 t. baking powder
1/2 t. baking soda

1 t. salt
2 eggs, beaten
1 c. light sour cream
1/4 c. butter, melted

In a bowl, combine cornmeal, flour, sugar, baking powder, baking soda
and salt; mix well and set aside. In another bowl, stir together eggs,
sour cream and melted butter. Add cornmeal mixture to egg mixture; stir
until moistened. Spoon batter into 12 well-greased muffin cups. Bake at
425 degrees for 15 to 20 minutes, until golden. Makes one dozen.

Christmas
for Sharing

Nancy & Harry's Chili

Nancy Kaiser
York, SC

This chili is very tasty, without a lot of heat. My husband enjoys making this early in the day and letting it simmer until it's time to eat. It's always better the next day if you have leftovers. It's delicious served with cheese, sour cream and tortilla chips.

1 lb. ground beef
1/2 c. onion, diced
28-oz. can diced tomatoes
14-1/2 oz. can zesty chili-style
   diced tomatoes
15-1/2 oz. can Mexican chili
   beans

6-oz. can tomato sauce
1/3 c. brown sugar, packed
1 T. chili powder
1 t. ground cumin
1 t. garlic powder
1/2 t. salt

Brown beef with onion in a large kettle over medium heat; drain. Stir in undrained tomatoes, undrained beans and remaining ingredients; bring to a boil. Reduce heat to medium-low. Simmer for at least 15 minutes, until ready to serve. Makes 6 to 8 servings.

For the sweetest family times, snuggle under a cozy throw and read favorite Christmas story books together. Young children will love being read to, while older kids may enjoy taking turns reading aloud from "*The Night before Christmas*" or "*A Christmas Carol.*"

Winter Warming
Soups & Breads

Southwest Chicken Chili

Teresa Warkentin
Hutchinson, KS

This flavorful chili is ready in a jiffy! Serve with corn chips and shredded Cheddar cheese on top.

1 T. oil
1 lb. boneless, skinless chicken
    breasts, cut into bite-size
    cubes
1/2 c. onion, chopped
2 15-1/2 oz. cans Great Northern
    beans, drained and rinsed

10-oz. can diced tomatoes with
    green chiles
14-1/2 oz. can chicken broth
1 t. ground cumin

Heat oil in a large saucepan over medium heat; add chicken and onion. Cook until chicken is cooked through, stirring occasionally. Stir in beans, tomatoes with juice, chicken broth and cumin; bring to a boil. Reduce heat to medium-low. Simmer for 10 minutes, stirring occasionally. Serves 6.

Ladle leftover soup into plastic containers in individual portions, label and freeze. On snowy days, everyone can pick their favorites to heat & eat in a jiffy.

Christmas
for Sharing

Shrimp Turmeric Stew

Courtney Stultz
Weir, KS

This stew features great veggies and shrimp with a bold, yet light turmeric sauce. Turmeric is said to have great nutritional properties, but we just love the flavor! It's great any time of year.

1 lb. small or medium shrimp,
   peeled and cleaned
3 c. vegetable, chicken or
   seafood broth
2 c. cabbage, chopped
1 chayote squash or yellow
   squash, peeled and diced
1 zucchini, diced
1 c. carrots, peeled and diced

1 baking potato, peeled and diced
1 small jalapeño pepper, seeded
   and diced
1 lime, cut into quarters
1 T. fresh cilantro, finely chopped
1 t. ground turmeric
1 t. sea salt
1/2 t. pepper

Combine all ingredients in a large stockpot over medium heat. Bring to a boil; reduce heat to medium-low. Cover and simmer for about 35 to 40 minutes, until vegetables are soft. Ingredients may also be combined in a 5-quart slow cooker; cover and cook on high setting for 4 hours, or on low setting for 8 hours. Makes 4 servings.

Make some quick & easy fire starters for a frosty winter day. Bundle newspaper into 6-inch squares and secure with natural twine. To use, tuck under firewood and light with a match.

Winter Warming
Soups & Breads

Easy Fish Stew

Lynda Robson
Boston, MA

A family favorite on blustery days. Serve with crackers or crusty bread for dipping into the flavorful broth.

6 T. extra-virgin olive oil
1-1/2 c. onion, chopped
3 cloves garlic, minced
2/3 c. fresh parsley, chopped
14-1/2 oz. can whole or
    crushed tomatoes
2 t. tomato paste
8-oz. bottle clam juice
1/2 c. dry white wine or water

1/8 t. dried oregano
1/8 t. dried thyme
1 t. salt
1/8 t. pepper
1-1/2 lbs. cod, flounder or
    haddock fillets, cut into
    2-inch cubes
1/8 t. hot pepper sauce,
    or to taste

Heat olive oil in a large soup pot over medium-high heat. Add onion and sauté for 4 minutes. Add garlic; cook for one minute. Add parsley; cook and stir for 2 minutes. Add tomatoes with juice and tomato paste; simmer over low heat for 10 minutes. Stir in remaining ingredients except fish and hot sauce; bring to a simmer. Add fish. Simmer over low heat for 3 to 5 minutes, until fish is cooked through and flakes easily. Stir in hot sauce and serve. Makes 4 servings.

Jazz up hot soup with savory herbed croutons! Heat one tablespoon olive oil in a large skillet; add a big spoonful of chopped fresh thyme, oregano or tarragon. Stir in 2 slices of bread, cubed. Cook, stirring occasionally, until lightly golden on all sides. Cool and sprinkle over soup.

Christmas
for Sharing

Holiday Cranberry Bread

Judy Phelan
Macomb, IL

*A holiday favorite bread, served at Christmas dinner. This recipe
can also be made in three mini loaf pans for gift giving...
just wrap up the loaves and add a ribbon bow!*

2 c. all-purpose flour
1-1/2 t. baking powder
1/2 t. baking soda
1/2 t. salt
1 c. sugar
1 egg, well beaten

2 T. butter, melted
2 T. hot water
1/4 c. orange zest
1/2 c. orange juice
1 c. dried cranberries
1/2 c. chopped pecans or walnuts

In a large bowl, combine flour, baking powder, baking soda and salt;
mix well. Add sugar, egg, butter, hot water, orange zest and juice; stir
until moistened. Fold in cranberries and nuts. Batter will be thick. Spoon
into a greased 9"x5" loaf pan or three, 5"x3" mini loaf pans. Bake at
325 degrees for 50 minutes, or 35 minutes for mini loaves. Cool; wrap
and refrigerate or freeze. Makes one loaf.

A holiday tea towel is a quick & easy wrap-up for a plastic-wrapped
loaf of fruit bread. Place the loaf in the center and bring the corners
together. Secure with a length of ribbon and you're done!

Seasonal
Sides & Salads

Christmas
for Sharing

Stuffing in a Bundt Pan

Joan Chance
Houston, TX

This stuffing is so good for a holiday dinner. It's easy to serve and looks special with cranberry sauce spooned into the center.

1 loaf French or ciabatta bread, cut into 1-inch cubes
1/2 c. butter
1 c. onion, chopped
3 stalks celery, chopped
4 eggs, beaten
1-1/2 c. chicken broth

1/4 c. fresh parsley, chopped
1 t. ground sage
3/4 t. salt
1/4 t. pepper
Optional: favorite cranberry sauce

Divide bread cubes between 2 baking sheets sprayed with non-stick vegetable spray. Bake at 375 degrees for 15 to 20 minutes, until toasted, stirring halfway through. Meanwhile, melt butter in a skillet over high heat. Sauté onion and celery for 8 to 10 minutes, until soft. In a large bowl, mix together eggs, chicken broth, parsley and seasonings. Add onion mixture and bread cubes; gently toss until thoroughly mixed. Spoon mixture into a Bundt® pan sprayed with non-stick spray; using spoon, press down into pan. Bake, uncovered, at 375 degrees for 40 to 45 minutes, until golden. Let stand for 5 minutes; turn out onto a serving plate. If desired, fill center of stuffing with cranberry sauce. Serves 8.

Vintage salt & pepper shakers add a touch of holiday cheer
to any table and a smile to guests' faces.

Seasonal
Sides & Salads

Spiced Christmas
Cranberry Sauce

Jennifer Smith
Kissimmee, FL

I have always loved cranberry sauce and I make it every year. I enjoy its tangy sweetness and vibrant red color...it just enhances all of my savory holiday dishes. In this recipe, I used honey and cider for the sweetness, and to make it a bit healthier. Plus, my daughter loves anything with honey in it! Your home will smell amazing while the sauce is simmering.

12-oz. pkg. fresh cranberries
1 c. apple cider
2 mandarin oranges, peeled
   and sectioned

1/2 c. honey
1 t. pumpkin pie spice
1 c. chopped pecans
1 t. vanilla extract

In a large saucepan over medium heat, combine cranberries and cider. Simmer until cranberries all pop and are the texture you prefer; do not drain. Meanwhile, in a bowl, chop orange sections into small bits, using a pastry cutter or food processor. Stir in honey and spice; add pecans and stir well. Add orange mixture to cooked cranberries; blend together well. Mix in vanilla. Simmer over low heat for about 30 minutes, stirring occasionally. Mixture will have a lot of liquid at first, but will thicken as it simmers. Transfer to a serving dish; cover and chill until serving time. Serves 10 to 12.

Trace around favorite cookie cutters onto colorful paper
for placecards and package tags...add glitter for sparkle.
Or make simple ornaments...trace onto doubled felt and
cut out, then blanket-stitch together and stuff lightly.

Christmas
for Sharing

Cindy's Potatoes Romanoff

Georgia Muth
Penn Valley, CA

My friend Cindy shared this recipe with me many years ago. It is a nice change from plain mashed potatoes. I serve it with prime rib or any roast meat. Baking the potatoes a day ahead shortens prep time when putting the dish together.

4 russet potatoes
3 shallots, minced
2-1/2 c. shredded white Cheddar
   cheese, divided

1 t. salt
1/4 t. white pepper
1-1/2 c. sour cream
1/2 c. grated Parmesan cheese

Pierce holes in potatoes with a fork; wrap in aluminum foil. Bake at 425 degrees for one hour, or until fork tender. Unwrap potatoes and let cool. Once cool, refrigerate for 4 hours or overnight. Do not peel potatoes. Grate potatoes, using the large holes on grater. In a large bowl, combine potatoes, shallots, 1-3/4 cups Cheddar cheese, salt and pepper; fold in sour cream. Transfer to a lightly greased 8"x8" baking pan; sprinkle with remaining Cheddar cheese and Parmesan cheese. Bake, uncovered, at 350 degrees for 30 minutes, or until hot and lightly golden. Makes 6 servings.

For a sweet placecard guests can take home, write each person's
name on a vintage Christmas postcard, then clip onto
the side of the dinner plate.

Seasonal
Sides & Salads

Creamy Asparagus Bake

Bethi Hendrickson
Danville, PA

This recipe comes from my grandmother's old Grange cookbook from the 1940s...it's so easy and so good!

1 lb. fresh asparagus spears, trimmed
2 T. butter
2 T. all-purpose flour
1 c. milk
1 t. lemon juice

3-oz. pkg. cream cheese, room temperature, cubed
1/2 c. soft bread crumbs
2 T. butter, melted
1/4 t. nutmeg

Cook asparagus in a skillet of water over medium heat; drain well. Arrange asparagus in a greased 2-quart casserole dish; set aside. Melt butter in a saucepan over medium heat; blend in flour, milk and lemon juice. Blend in cream cheese; spoon mixture over asparagus. Toss together bread crumbs and melted butter; sprinkle on top. Sprinkle with nutmeg. Bake, uncovered, at 350 degrees for 30 minutes. Serves 4 to 5.

Katie's Famous Green Beans

Katie Bonomo
Danville, IL

Fresh green beans are best, but when I can't get them, I use this slow-cooker recipe and nobody can tell the difference!

1 c. onion, chopped
1 to 2 T. garlic, minced
2 T. butter
1/4 c. bacon drippings

3 10-oz. pkgs. frozen green beans
3 c. chicken broth

In a skillet over medium heat, sauté onion and garlic in butter. Transfer mixture and remaining ingredients to a 6-quart slow cooker. Cover and cook on high setting for 4 to 5 hours, or on low setting for 6 to 8 hours. Makes 10 servings.

The more the merrier! Why not invite a neighbor or a college student who might be spending the holiday alone to share the Christmas feast with you?

Christmas
for Sharing

Sweet Potato Logs

Joyce Roebuck
Jacksonville, TX

*A fun and tasty change from the usual Thanksgiving
sweet potato casserole.*

4 sweet potatoes, peeled,
   quartered and cooked
1 c. sugar
1 egg, beaten
1/4 c. milk
3 T. plus 1 t. all-purpose flour,
   divided

1 t. vanilla extract
1 t. cinnamon
1/2 c. chopped pecans
1/2 c. raisins
1 c. flaked coconut
1/2 c. butter, melted

Mash sweet potatoes in a large bowl. Add sugar, egg, milk, 3 tablespoons
flour, vanilla, cinnamon and pecans; mix well and set aside. Toss raisins
in remaining flour; add to sweet potato mixture, mixing well. Cool;
shape mixture into 8 logs or croquettes. Roll logs in coconut. Arrange
on a lightly greased baking sheet; drizzle with melted butter. Bake at
375 degrees for about 20 minutes, until crisp and golden. Makes
8 servings.

Tame those loose spools of ribbon...just place them
on an upright paper towel holder!

Seasonal
Sides & Salads

Bok Choy Salad

Janis Parr
Ontario, Canada

*This is a delicious and healthy salad that's just a little different.
I get requests for it whenever there is a potluck.*

4 heads baby bok choy, chopped,
   including stems
2 green onions, chopped
3-oz. pkg. chicken ramen
   noodles, divided
1/3 c. slivered almonds

1/4 c. butter
1/2 c. sugar
1/4 c. oil
1/4 c. white vinegar
1 T. soy sauce

Combine bok choy and onions in a large bowl; set aside. Break up ramen noodles into smaller pieces; reserve seasoning packet for another use. In a skillet over medium heat, cook noodles and almonds in butter until golden; set aside to cool. For dressing, combine remaining ingredients; stir well until sugar dissolves. Just before serving, add dressing mixture to noodle mixture; stir well. Add to bok choy mixture and stir to coat well. Serve immediately. Makes 6 to 8 servings.

Get together with friends for a Christmas craft night. Ask each friend to bring along an idea and simple supplies to share. It's such fun to make note cards, gift tags and ornaments together!

Christmas
for Sharing

Spinach Salad

Barbara Klein
Newburgh, IN

This is a wonderful salad with a delicious homemade French dressing. For variety, sliced mushrooms, sliced strawberries and/or mandarin oranges may be added.

1-1/2 lbs. fresh spinach, torn
2 to 3 eggs, hard-boiled, peeled and chopped
2 to 3 slices bacon, crisply cooked and crumbled

2.8-oz. can French fried onions
1 to 1-1/2 c. shredded mozzarella cheese
8 to 12 t. sunflower seeds

Make French Dressing; set aside or chill. At serving time, divide spinach among 4 to 6 individual salad plates. Sprinkle with remaining ingredients, as desired. Serve with dressing. Makes 4 to 6 servings.

French Dressing:

3/4 c. oil
1/2 c. vinegar
1 c. sugar
1/4 c. onion, grated

1/4 c. catsup
2 t. paprika
2 t. salt

Combine all ingredients in a blender; process until smooth.

Gather up the neighbor kids and go caroling...just for the joy of singing together! Type up lyrics to favorite carols and make enough copies for everyone. You're sure to have a great time.

Seasonal
Sides & Salads

Friend's Au Gratin Potatoes

Janet Dolbow
West Deptford, NJ

Our friend Tom, who has since passed away, used to make these potatoes for us when we ate over. He didn't have any measurements, just told me what to put in. So I fiddled with them until I got the measurements the way I wanted and even tweaked them a bit. My family loves them.

6 Red Bliss potatoes, thinly sliced
1 c. butter
1/4 c. all-purpose flour
2 t. onion powder
1 t. garlic powder
1/4 t. pepper
8-oz. pkg. sharp Cooper cheese,
   shredded

Arrange potato slices in a greased 2-quart deep casserole dish; set side. Melt butter in a saucepan over medium-low heat. Add flour and seasonings; cook and stir until thickened. Add cheese; cook and stir until melted. Spoon over potatoes in dish. Bake, uncovered, at 350 degrees for one hour, or until hot and golden. Serves 8.

MiMi's Peppered Potatoes

Glenda Ballard
West Columbia, SC

A Friday night favorite at our house! We love the peppery large chunks of potatoes and onion. It's usually enjoyed with ham and baked beans.

1/4 to 1/3 c. oil
4 potatoes, peeled and cut into
   bite-size cubes
1 large onion, cut into
   bite-size cubes
1/2 t. salt
1/2 t. pepper
1/3 c. water

Spread oil in a pot over medium-high heat. Test for readiness by adding one cube each of potato and onion; if it sizzles, add remaining potatoes and onion. Add salt and pepper; stir until vegetables are well coated with oil. Sauté just until oil is absorbed. Reduce heat to low; add water. Cover and simmer for 15 to 20 minutes, stirring occasionally. Check for doneness; simmer an additional 3 minutes, if needed. Serves 4 to 5.

Christmas
for Sharing

Parmesan-Roasted Broccoli

Ann Farris
Biscoe, AR

We live in a rural area, where we've learned to work with what is available. That's where this recipe came from...use what you have!

6 to 7 c. broccoli, cut into
    bite-size flowerets
3 to 4 T. olive oil
1/4 c. Italian-seasoned dry
    bread crumbs

1/2 c. shredded Parmesan cheese
1 t. dried, minced garlic
salt and pepper to taste
8 to 10 slices bacon, crisply
    cooked and crumbled

Combine broccoli and olive oil in a large plastic zipping bag; shake to coat well. Add bread crumbs, Parmesan cheese and seasonings to bag; shake to coat. With your hands, rub the bag to help the coating to stick to the broccoli. Line a rimmed baking sheet with aluminum foil; spray with non-stick vegetable spray. Spread broccoli mixture evenly on baking sheet; top with crumbled bacon. Bake at 425 degrees for 12 minutes; stir. Bake another 10 to 15 minutes, until broccoli is tender. Serves 5.

Sing we all merrily, Christmas is here,
The day we love best of all days in the year!
–Old English poem

Seasonal
Sides & Salads

Roasted Baby Carrots

Alice Schnelle
Oak Lawn, IL

Best carrots you have ever tasted! Bake the carrots after you've removed your roast from the oven and set it aside to rest, or bake them at the same time as your roast, if you have the oven space.

1-1/2 lbs. baby carrots
6 whole cloves garlic
2 T. butter, sliced into 6 pats

6 sprigs fresh thyme
salt and cracked pepper to taste
1 c. white wine or chicken broth

Tear a large sheet of aluminum foil which can be doubled and sealed like a pouch; place on a rimmed baking sheet. Add carrots and other ingredients in order listed. Roll all edges of foil to seal like a pouch. Bake at 400 degrees for 35 to 40 minutes, until carrots are tender. Serves 6.

Old-Fashioned Harvard Beets

Teresa Verell
Roanoke, VA

This recipe is always requested for Christmas dinner. Everyone loves these tangy beets!

1/2 c. sugar
1/3 c. white wine vinegar
1/3 c. water
4 t. cornstarch

2 15-oz. cans sliced beets,
 well drained
3 T. butter

In a saucepan over medium heat, combine sugar, vinegar, water and cornstarch. Bring to a boil; simmer for 5 minutes. Reduce heat to low. Add beets; simmer for 30 minutes. Stir in butter. Remove from heat and serve warm. Serves 6.

Tuck a string of tiny white lights
into a flower arrangement
for extra sparkle.

Christmas
for Sharing

Tangy Pea Salad

Jacki Smith
Fayetteville, NC

My family & friends always ask for this salad at Thanksgiving, Christmas, Easter and other special occasions. It's a holiday tradition for us! It's a potluck favorite as well. Great with baked ham, barbecue or chicken salad sandwiches. It is easy to make ahead of time, and keeps in the refrigerator for up to a week.

15-oz. can very young peas, drained
15-oz. can white shoepeg corn, drained
14-1/2 oz. can cut green beans, drained

4-oz. sliced mushrooms, drained
2-oz. jar sliced pimentos, drained
1 green pepper, chopped
1 onion, chopped

Make Syrup; set aside to cool. In a large bowl, combine all vegetables and cooled syrup. Toss to mix well. Cover and refrigerate overnight before serving. Serves 10 to 12.

Syrup:

1 c. sugar
1 c. oil
1/2 c. cider vinegar

2 t. salt
2 t. pepper

Combine all ingredients in a microwave-safe bowl. Microwave on high for 2 minutes, or until sugar dissolves.

Christmas waves a magic wand over this world, and behold, everything is softer and more beautiful.

–Norman Vincent Peale

Seasonal
Sides & Salads

Holiday Fruit Salad

Dawn Nolan
Lake Charles, LA

This salad has been on the Thanksgiving and Christmas buffet table in my family for four generations. Sometimes it is still warm here in Louisiana during Thanksgiving and Christmas, so it's nice to have a cool fruit salad on the menu.

2 apples, cored and cubed
2 bananas, sliced
2 15-oz. cans fruit cocktail,
    partially drained
11-oz. can mandarin oranges,
    partially drained

8-oz. can pineapple chunks,
    partially drained
14-oz. can sweetened condensed
    milk
1 c. pecans, coarsely chopped

Combine all fruits in a large serving bowl. Add condensed milk and stir. Add pecans and stir gently. Cover and refrigerate until ready to serve. Makes 10 to 12 servings.

A sweet family tradition! Begin a Christmas scrapbook and fill it with copies of letters to Santa, wish lists and holiday photos...what fun to read and add to, year after year.

Christmas
for Sharing

Mama's Oyster Dressing

*Ruth Conroy
Anderson, IN*

This is an old-fashioned dressing with giblets, very tasty and very comforting. It makes enough to stuff a 12 to 15-pound turkey.

1 loaf day-old white bread
giblets from one turkey
1-1/2 c. water
1/4 c. butter
1 pt. fresh oysters, drained
    and liquid reserved

1 c. onion, chopped
7 stalks celery, chopped
2 t. chicken bouillon powder
2 T. poultry seasoning
1 T. salt
2 eggs, beaten

Place bread slices in a single layer on 2 to 3 baking sheets. Bake at 350 degrees for 15 minutes, or until dried out; cut into one-inch squares and set aside. Meanwhile, add giblets and water to a small saucepan. Cook over medium-low heat until tender; cool and chop. Melt butter in another saucepan; add oysters, onion and celery. Cook over low heat until vegetables are tender. Stir in bouillon powder, poultry seasoning and salt. In a large bowl, combine oyster mixture, giblets with broth and bread cubes; stir in eggs. Transfer to a greased 13"x9" deep baking pan; cover with aluminum foil. Bake at 350 degrees for 30 minutes, or until heated through. Let cool before serving. Serves 8 to 10.

Tuck battery-operated tealights and pillar candles
into favorite votives, sconces and centerpieces
for a safe, soft glow.

Seasonal
Sides & Salads

Winter Sweet Potato Soufflé

Edward Kielar
Whitehouse, OH

A family favorite for holidays, easy and yet so special.
Potatoes can be made ahead of time. The topping should be
put on just before baking.

40-oz. can sweet potatoes,
   drained
1/2 c. butter, softened
3/4 c. sugar

3 eggs, beaten
1/2 c. milk
1 t. vanilla extract
1/8 t. salt

Mash sweet potatoes in a large bowl; add remaining ingredients. Beat
with an electric mixer on medium speed until smooth. Spoon into a
greased 2-quart casserole dish, no more than 2 inches deep. Sprinkle
Topping over sweet potato mixture. Bake, uncovered, at 350 degrees
for 40 minutes, or until heated through. Serves 8.

Topping:

3/4 c. brown sugar, packed
1/2 c. butter, softened

1/2 c. self-rising flour
1 c. chopped pecans

Combine all ingredients; mix well.

A pocket calendar for the new year makes a thoughtful gift
for family members near & far. Fill in birthdays, anniversaries
and other important dates...sure to be appreciated
and used, all year 'round!

Christmas
for Sharing

JoAnn's Best Green Bean Casserole Ever

Kelly Serdynski
Hedgesville, WV

My mom has made this casserole for us for every birthday, Thanksgiving and Christmas. This casserole means a special occasion, company is coming, or it's holiday time. We've even heated it up for breakfast on Christmas morning, it's so good! The nicest part is, you can make it ahead of time and pop it in the refrigerator until you're ready to bake.

2 14-1/2 oz. cans French-cut
   green beans, drained
15-oz. can white shoepeg corn,
   drained
1/2 c. celery, thinly sliced
1/2 c. onion, finely diced
1/4 c. green pepper, finely diced
1 c. shredded Cheddar cheese
1 c. sour cream

10-3/4 oz. can cream of
   celery soup
1-1/2 t. salt
1 t. pepper
1 sleeve buttery round crackers,
   crushed
1/2 c. slivered almonds
1/2 c. butter, sliced

In a large bowl, combine all vegetables, cheese, sour cream, celery soup, salt and pepper; mix well. Transfer to a lightly greased 13"x9" baking pan; flatten mixture with spoon. In another bowl, combine crackers and almonds; sprinkle over casserole. Dot with butter. Bake, uncovered, at 350 degrees for 45 minutes, or until hot and bubbly. Serves 8.

Santa's little helpers will enjoy snipping designs out of last year's Christmas cards. Once they're cut, glue onto store-bought cards or handmade gift tags that add charm to every package!

Seasonal
Sides & Salads

Yellow Rice Pilaf

Kristin Pittis
Dennison, OH

This super-easy rice is even better than the pre-packaged version.
It's healthier too, with added veggies and no preservatives.

2 t. olive oil
1/2 onion, diced
1 c. long-grain white rice,
   uncooked
1/2 t. garlic powder
1/2 t. onion powder

1/2 t. ground turmeric
1/2 t. dried basil
1 t. salt
2 c. chicken broth
1 c. frozen pea & carrot blend

Heat oil in a skillet over medium heat. Add onion and cook for
3 minutes. Add rice and seasonings; stir until combined and sauté
for 2 minutes. Stir in chicken broth and bring to a boil. Reduce heat to
medium-low; cover and simmer for 10 minutes. Stir in peas and carrots;
cover and cook an additional 10 minutes, or until rice is tender. Fluff
with a fork before serving. Makes 6 servings.

Keep a variety of bagged fresh salads in the crisper. Tossed with
dried cranberries, bacon bits, cheese cubes or croutons and
a simple dressing, salads can be made to order in no time at all.

Christmas
for Sharing

Holiday Greens

Myrtle Miller
Providence, KY

A perfect side for baked ham or roast turkey, passed down at least three generations. I believe hard-boiled eggs were added during lean times to provide protein when little was available. It makes a lot!

2 to 3 cubes chicken or
   beef bouillon
1 c. boiling water
8 to 10 slices bacon
2 onions, chopped
12 c. collard greens, chopped

1-1/2 t. cider vinegar
2 t. sugar, or more to taste
salt and pepper to taste
7 to 8 eggs, hard-boiled, peeled
   and chopped

Combine bouillon cubes and boiling water in a cup; set aside. In a large stockpot over medium heat, cook bacon until crisp. Remove bacon to paper towels to drain; reserve 2 to 3 tablespoons drippings in pot. Add onions to pot; cook for 2 to 3 minutes. Gradually add collard greens; continue cooking and stirring for 10 to 15 minutes, until collards are all added and are tender. Stir bouillon mixture; add to greens along with vinegar. If mixture looks too dry, add a little more water. Season with sugar, salt and pepper. Add crumbled bacon and chopped eggs; stir to mix in evenly. Makes 24 servings.

Can't find the perfect gift for Auntie, Sis or that extra-special friend? Why not invite her to a leisurely lunch at a favorite restaurant after Christmas, when you'll both have more time for chatting over coffee. She'll enjoy your thoughtfulness!

Seasonal
Sides & Salads

Anytime Zucchini Salad

JoAnna Nicoline-Haughey
Berwyn, PA

A simple way to enjoy that fresh-grown, farmers' market-fresh garden zucchini. Great for gatherings!

4 zucchini, thinly sliced
2 14-oz. cans artichoke hearts, drained
2 4-oz. cans sliced black olives, drained
8-oz. can bamboo shoots, drained
8-oz. can sliced mushrooms, drained
8-oz. bottle Italian salad dressing
1-oz. pkg. ranch salad dressing mix

Combine all ingredients in a large bowl; toss to mix well. Cover and refrigerate overnight before serving. Serves 6 to 8.

Honey-Baked Onions

Gladys Kielar
Whitehouse, OH

The best onions ever!

6 sweet onions, peeled, trimmed and halved
1-1/2 c. tomato juice
1-1/2 c. water
2 T. honey
2 T. butter, melted

Arrange onion halves in a buttered 13"x9" baking pan, cut-side down; set aside. Stir together remaining ingredients in a bowl; spoon over onions. Bake, uncovered, at 325 degrees for one hour, or until onions are soft. Serves 6.

Sort through your family's closets and donate gently worn and outgrown coats, clothes and extra blankets to a nearby shelter. They'll be much appreciated, and you'll be making space for new items.

Christmas
for Sharing

Escarole & Pear Salad

Carolyn Deckard
Bedford, IN

This salad was a hit at our ladies' get-together from work! It's one of my favorite ways of fixing pears, so easy and so delicious.

3 c. escarole or leaf lettuce, torn
2 pears, cored and thinly sliced

1 T. chopped hazelnuts

Make Dressing; set aside. Divide escarole or lettuce among 6 individual salad plates. Arrange pear slices over lettuce; sprinkle with hazelnuts. Drizzle with dressing and serve immediately. Makes 6 servings.

Dressing:

3 T. cider vinegar
3 T. raspberry jam

1 T. oil

Combine all ingredients in a small jar with a lid. Add lid and shake until well mixed.

Toasted nuts give tossed salads extra flavor and crunch. Add chopped nuts to a small dry skillet. Cook and stir over low heat for a few minutes, until toasty and golden. Let cool before adding to salads.

Seasonal
Sides & Salads

Kerri's Party Pasta Salad

Sandy Coffey
Cincinnati, OH

My daughter Kerri makes this pasta salad for all of our family gatherings...Christmas, Easter, Fourth of July, Halloween, birthdays, anytime! With lots of yummy veggies, great flavor and bright colors, it's always a big hit. Choose your pepper colors according to the season or event.

16-oz. pkg. rotini pasta,
    uncooked
4 assorted green, red, yellow
    and/or orange peppers, diced
1 bunch broccoli, cut into
    bite-size flowerets
1 head cauliflower, cut into
    bite-size flowerets

1 cucumber, cubed
1 pt. cherry tomatoes
3-1/2 oz. pkg. sliced pepperoni
1 to 2 8-oz. bottles ranch salad
    dressing

Cook pasta according to package directions; drain and rinse with cold water. Combine pasta and remaining ingredients in a large bowl, adding desired amount of salad dressing; mix well. Cover and refrigerate for 2 hours to overnight. Stir well at serving time. Makes 10 to 15 servings.

For the tastiest pasta salads, stir in a little more dressing after removing from the fridge. A sprinkle of fresh-chopped herbs is an extra-special touch. Allow salad to stand at room temperature for several minutes, just enough to take the chill off. Sure to become a favorite!

Christmas
for Sharing

Cranberry-Pineapple Gelatin Salad

Jenny Maggio
Van Nuys, CA

I've made this salad for Christmas Eve. It's very good and goes well with a pork roast. Will keep, refrigerated, for several days.

20-oz. can crushed pineapple, very well drained and juice reserved
6-oz. pkg. raspberry gelatin mix
2/3 c. walnuts, coarsely chopped

15-oz. can whole-berry cranberry sauce
1 green apple, peeled, cored and chopped

In a saucepan, combine reserved pineapple juice and enough water to equal 2-1/2 cups. Bring to a boil over high heat; add gelatin. Cook and stir for 2 minutes, or until dissolved. Stir in remaining ingredients; pour into a 13"x9" glass baking pan. Cover and chill for 2-1/2 hours, or until set. Serves 10 to 12.

Lime Gelatin Salad

Darla Cottom
Terre Haute, IN

This is made every Thanksgiving and Christmas for my family.

3-oz. pkg. lime gelatin mix
1 c. boiling water
8-oz. pkg. cream cheese, softened
1 T. sugar

1 t. vanilla extract
8-oz. can crushed pineapple, drained
1 c. lemon-lime soda

In a large bowl, dissolve gelatin mix in boiling water. Stir in cream cheese; beat until smooth. Stir in sugar, vanilla and pineapple; stir in soda. Transfer to a 9"x9" glass baking pan. Cover and refrigerate until firm; cut into squares. Makes 12 servings.

Dress up gelatin salads with a dollop of creamy lemon mayonnaise. Stir 3 tablespoons each of lemon juice, light cream and powdered sugar into 1/2 cup mayonnaise...done!

Seasonal
Sides & Salads

Pineapple Dressing

Deborah Hassfurther
Ferdinand, IN

This pineapple dressing has been enjoyed by my family for 30 years, especially with baked ham. It's scrumptious as either a side dish or as a dessert.

1 c. butter, room temperature
14-oz. can sweetened
   condensed milk
4 c. sugar

4 eggs, beaten
2 20-oz. cans pineapple chunks
2 loaves white bread, torn into
   small pieces

Combine butter, condensed milk, sugar and eggs in a very large bowl; beat well. Add pineapple with juice; mix well. Fold in bread cubes; mix well. Transfer to a greased 13"x9" baking pan. Bake, uncovered, at 350 degrees for 40 to 45 minutes, until center thickens and edges are golden. Don't overbake! Makes 8 to 10 servings.

Mother's 5-Cup Salad

Pat Prater
Munford, TN

My mother made this recipe for the first time one Christmas when I was about 15 years old; I am now in my 70s. Our family loves it, and it is only made at Christmas. We have carried 5-Cup Salad through all the years and will have it this Christmas too...enjoy!

1 c. sour cream
1 c. mini marshmallows
1 c. crushed pineapple, drained

1 c. mandarin oranges, drained
1 c. sweetened shredded coconut

Mix together all ingredients in a large bowl. Cover and refrigerate for at least 4 hours before serving. Makes 6 servings.

Light a scented candle just before guests arrive, for a fragrant welcome after a long drive.

Christmas
for Sharing

Letha's Candy Cabbage

Judy Gillham
Whittier, CA

This is my grandmother's recipe. It was one of my daughter's favorites as a child, a German-inspired, attractive, full-of-flavor side dish. It's perfect to serve with hearty meats in the cold winter.

2 T. bacon drippings
4 c. red cabbage, coarsely
   shredded
2 tart apples, peeled, cored
   and quartered
10 whole cloves

1/2 c. boiling water
1/4 c. brown sugar, packed
2 T. cider vinegar
1 t. all-purpose flour
1/4 t. cinnamon
salt and pepper to taste

Heat bacon drippings in a Dutch oven or other large pot. Add cabbage, apples and cloves; pour boiling water over all. Simmer over medium-low heat until tender, about 45 minutes. Combine remaining ingredients except salt and pepper in a small bowl. Add to cooked cabbage mixture and stir well. Cook and stir for 5 more minutes, until slightly thickened. Season with salt and pepper as desired; serve hot. Makes 8 servings.

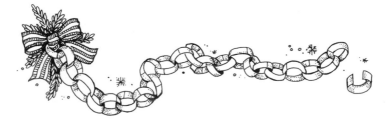

Make a happiness chain to wind around the tree. Cut strips of colorful paper and have family members write a few words on each strip about what makes them feel happy..."my cat Fluffy," "making snow angels" and so on. Tape strips together into loops to form a chain...sure to bring smiles!

Seasonal
Sides & Salads

Turkey in the Slaw

Sherry Sheehan
Evensville, TX

*The basic part of this recipe is my mom's own coleslaw recipe.
I adapted it for the holidays by adding leftover roast turkey,
dried cranberries and pecans. It's delicious!*

1 c. mayonnaise
3/8 c. sugar
2 T. cider vinegar
1 t. salt
1/8 t. pepper

16-oz. pkg. shredded
   coleslaw mix
2 c. cooked turkey, diced
1/3 c. dried cranberries
1/2 c. chopped pecans

In a large serving dish, combine mayonnaise, sugar, vinegar, salt
and pepper; stir well. Stir in coleslaw mix, a little at a time; fold in
turkey, cranberries and pecans. Cover and chill until serving time.
Makes 8 servings.

Turn a favorite hearty salad into a sandwich...
just stuff it into pita pockets! Add some chips and
pickles for a tasty hand-held meal.

Christmas
for Sharing

Sweet & Spicy Roasted Vegetables *Courtney Stultz*
Weir, KS

Our favorite way to eat winter vegetables is roasting them.
This recipe features a variety of spices to give a slightly spicy,
yet sweet flavor that goes well with many dishes.

2 c. butternut squash, peeled
   and diced
1 c. carrots, peeled and diced
1 c. parsnips, peeled and diced
1 c. apples, peeled, cored
   and diced
1/4 c. coconut oil

1 t. garlic, minced
1 t. cinnamon
1/2 t. paprika
1 t. sea salt
1/2 t. pepper
1/4 t. cayenne pepper

In a large bowl, toss squash, carrots, parsnips and apples with coconut
oil until coated. Spread evenly on a large rimmed baking sheet; sprinkle
with garlic and seasonings. Bake at 400 degrees for about 25 minutes,
until fork-tender, turning once during baking. Makes 4 to 6 servings.

Take the kids to a paint-your-own pottery shop.
They'll love decorating a plate and mug especially
for Santa's milk and cookies!

Seasonal
Sides & Salads

Pecan-Glazed Brussels Sprouts

Gladys Kielar
Whitehouse, OH

*Golden toasted pecans give Brussels sprouts an extra
festive crunch we love for holidays.*

1-1/2 lbs. Brussels sprouts,
   trimmed
1/2 c. water
1/4 c. butter
1/3 c. light brown sugar, packed

3 T. soy sauce
1/4 t. salt
1/2 c. toasted pecans,
   finely chopped

Cut a shallow X in the base of each Brussels sprout; set aside. Bring water to a boil in a large saucepan over medium heat; add sprouts. Reduce heat to medium-low. Cover and simmer for 10 minutes, or until sprouts are partially softened; drain and set aside. Melt butter in a skillet over medium heat; stir in brown sugar, soy sauce and salt. Bring to a boil, stirring constantly. Add pecans; reduce heat to medium-low. Simmer, uncovered, for 5 minutes, stirring often. Add sprouts to skillet; cook over medium heat for 5 minutes, or until softened. Stir well before serving. Serves 6.

Sprinkle a tossed green salad with ruby-red pomegranate
seeds for a festive touch.

Christmas
for Sharing

Loaded Potato Casserole

Jeana Owens
Cumberland Gap, TN

I make this dish for church dinners, family reunions and other special dinners...they all love it!

3-1/2 to 4 lbs. potatoes, peeled
   and quartered
1 T. plus 1 t. salt
1/2 c. cream cheese, room
   temperature
1/2 c. sour cream
1/4 c. butter, softened

1/2 t. pepper
1-1/2 c. shredded Cheddar
   cheese, divided
8 slices bacon, crisply cooked,
   chopped and divided
Optional: 1/2 bunch green
   onions, thinly sliced

Cover potatoes with water in a large saucepan. Cook over high heat until partially tender; drain. Add remaining ingredients, reserving 1/2 cup cheese, half of bacon and optional onions for topping. Stir all together; spoon into a lightly buttered 13"x9" baking pan. Bake, uncovered, at 375 degrees for 20 minutes. Remove from oven; top with reserved cheese, bacon and onions, if using. Return to oven and bake for another 5 minutes, or until cheese is melted. Makes 8 to 10 servings.

Try serving a colorful veggie tray with dinner, instead of a salad. Filled with crisp broccoli flowerets, cherry tomatoes, sweet pepper rings and cucumber slices, it's sure to have something for everyone. Add a cup of ranch salad dressing for delicious dipping...simple!

Seasonal
Sides & Salads

Red, White & Green Salad

Judy Phelan
Macomb, IL

A family recipe from years back.

2 bunches broccoli, cut into
    flowerets
1 head cauliflower, cut into
    flowerets
1 bunch green onions, diced

2 c. cherry tomatoes
1 c. mayonnaise
1/2 c. sour cream
1 T. vinegar
2 T. sugar

Combine all vegetables in a large bowl; set aside. In a separate bowl, combine remaining ingredients; blend well and spoon over vegetables. Mix until vegetables are well coated. Cover and refrigerate for 4 hours or more before serving. Serves 10 to 12.

Dollar stores can be gold mines for fun little stocking stuffers. Watch year 'round for tiny games, wind-up toys, mini bath products and hair ornaments...tuck your finds into a big well-hidden box. On Christmas Eve, you'll have lots of surprises to tuck into stockings!

Christmas
for Sharing

Oven-Roasted Potato Salad with Fennel

JoAnne Wilson
Roselle Park, NJ

Roasting potatoes instead of boiling brings out so much flavor. Several years ago, I roasted a lot of potatoes for a dinner party. I had so many left over, I mixed it up as potato salad. I didn't have any celery, but had a fennel bulb, and since then this is how I make it.

2 to 3 lbs. medium Yukon Gold
    potatoes, cubed
2 T. extra-virgin olive oil
1/2 t. Herbs de Provence,
    or to taste
salt and pepper to taste

1/8 to 1/4 t. hot Hungarian
    paprika
1 fennel bulb, peeled and very
    thinly sliced
1/2 to 1 c. mayonnaise

Place potatoes in a roasting pan. Drizzle evenly with olive oil; sprinkle all over with seasonings. Bake, uncovered, at 400 degrees for 25 to 30 minutes. Remove from oven; toss carefully. Return to oven for 10 to 15 minutes, until potatoes are tender but not mushy. Gently mix in fennel. Add desired amount of mayonnaise and mix gently. Season with additional salt and pepper, if desired. Cover and refrigerate until cooled completely, up to a day in advance. Makes 6 servings.

Christmas tree farms sometimes offer rides in horse-drawn sleighs or wagons...take the family for a ride they'll never forget! You may even be able to warm up afterwards with cups of hot cocoa or cider.

Seasonal
Sides & Salads

Baked Beans for 20

Shirl Parsons
Cape Carteret, NC

This recipe is one a dear friend of mine gave me a few years ago. Great for tailgating and other get-togethers!

7-lb. can pork & beans
1-3/4 c. onions, finely chopped
1-3/4 c. catsup
7/8 c. brown sugar, packed

3-1/2 T. mustard
12 to 14 slices bacon, partially
cooked and drained
Optional: green pepper rings

Add pork & beans to a large bowl; stir in onions, catsup, brown sugar and mustard. Transfer to a lightly greased 3-quart casserole dish. Arrange bacon slices on top. Bake, uncovered, at 350 degrees for 1-1/4 hours, or until bubbly. If desired, garnish with green pepper rings. Serves 20.

Slow-Cooker Mashed Potatoes

Lori Mulhern
Rosemount, MN

Can't have too many mashed potatoes! This recipe can be made the day before, saving a lot of time in the kitchen the next day before the big holiday meal. It is easy and so convenient. If you like, substitute chive cream cheese for a little extra flavor.

5 lbs. potatoes, peeled and
quartered
8-oz. pkg. cream cheese,
softened

1 c. butter, softened
1 c. sour cream
Garnish: chopped fresh chives

Cover potatoes with water in a large saucepan. Cook over high heat until fork-tender; drain. Mash potatoes in a large bowl. Add cream cheese, butter and sour cream; mix well. Transfer to a 5-quart slow cooker. Cover and cook on low setting for 3 hours. May be made the day before and refrigerated overnight; reheat before serving. Just before serving, garnish with chopped chives. Serves 10 to 12.

When cooking potatoes, add a chicken
bouillon cube or 2 to the water for extra flavor.

Christmas
for Sharing

Rice & Barley Salad

Pat Martin
Riverside, CA

I serve this delicious recipe as a holiday side dish. When my son was vegan, I just substituted vegetable broth for the chicken broth. The dressing ingredients can be doubled, which I like to do. This is a good make-ahead dish..any leftovers can be used to stuff pita bread the next day, too.

1-3/4 c. low-sodium fat-free
    chicken or vegetable broth
1/2 c. brown and wild rice mix,
    uncooked
1/2 c. pearled barley, uncooked

3/4 c. canned chickpeas, drained
    and rinsed
1/3 c. golden raisins
1/4 c. green onions, sliced
2 T. toasted sliced almonds

In a large saucepan, combine broth, rice mix and barley. Bring to a boil over medium-high heat. Reduce heat to medium-low; cover and and simmer for 30 to 40 minutes. Remove from heat; cover and let stand for 5 minutes. Transfer to a large bowl; add remaining ingredients. Add Dressing and toss. Cover and refrigerate for 2 hours or overnight. Serves 8.

Dressing:

2 T. red wine vinegar
1-1/2 t. extra-virgin olive oil
1 t. Dijon mustard

1/4 t. salt
1/4 t. pepper

Combine all ingredients in a jar with a lid; cover and shake well.

Just for fun, use a different color of wrapping paper for
each family member's gifts, but keep the colors
secret 'til it's time to unwrap them!

Sharing
Christmas
Together

Christmas
for Sharing

Christmas Confetti Tamales

Georgia Muth
Penn Valley, CA

A meal with tamales on Christmas Eve is a tradition in our family.
For leftovers, I add a few ingredients to make this different take
on tamale pie. The tamales can be found at most grocery stores.

8 cooked fresh or frozen pork or
  beef tamales
1-1/2 c. tamale or enchilada
  sauce
10-oz. can diced tomatoes with
  green chiles, drained

15-oz. can corn
3/4 c. canned creamed corn
Optional: 2.8-oz. can sliced black
  olives, drained
1-1/2 c. shredded Cheddar
  cheese, divided

Unwrap tamales and cut each into 6 to 8 pieces. Place tamale pieces
in a 13"x9" glass baking pan sprayed with non-stick vegetable spray.
Add remaining ingredients except cheese; mix gently. Sprinkle with
cheese. Cover with aluminum foil; bake at 375 degrees for 20 minutes.
Remove foil; bake for another 12 minutes, or until hot and bubbly.
Makes 8 servings.

For a quick and colorful centerpiece, curl a string of
dried chile peppers into a circle, then set a hurricane
with a fat red candle in the center.

Sharing Christmas *Together*

Chicken Parmesan Casserole

Norma Murphy
Orinda, CA

My family loves this chicken casserole anytime during the winter months, but especially on Christmas Eve. You could use chicken tenders and cut the baking time.

1/2 c. butter, melted
1 c. all-purpose flour
salt and pepper to taste
4 boneless, skinless chicken
   breasts

8-oz. pkg. sliced mushrooms
16-oz. container whipping cream
   or half-and-half
3/4 to 1 c. grated Parmesan
   cheese

Add melted butter to a shallow bowl. Place flour in another shallow bowl; season generously with salt and pepper. Dip chicken pieces into butter; dredge in flour mixture. Arrange chicken in a lightly greased 3-quart casserole dish; set aside. Add butter remaining in dish to a skillet; heat over medium heat. Add mushrooms and sauté lightly; spoon mushrooms over chicken. Add enough cream or half-and-half to nearly cover all ingredients. Top generously with Parmesan cheese. Cover and bake at 425 degrees for 30 minutes, or until heated through. Makes 4 servings.

Tuck a crock of garlic butter in the fridge, for hot garlic bread in a jiffy. Blend 1/2 cup softened butter, one teaspoon garlic powder, 1/2 teaspoon dried parsley and 1/4 teaspoon onion powder. Keep refrigerated. To use, spread on slices of Italian bread; broil until golden. Delicious!

Johnny Marzetti

LaDeana Cooper
Batavia, OH

A good old favorite that's worth revisiting. Whether the winter snow has you stranded in the house, experiencing lean times, or you just want a quick & easy meal, this one will become a staple in your house, as it has in mine.

16-oz. pkg. elbow macaroni,
  uncooked
2 lbs. ground beef
3/4 c. yellow onion, chopped
2 cloves garlic, minced
28-oz. can crushed tomatoes
29-oz. can tomato sauce

2 t. dried basil
1-1/2 t. dried oregano
1 T. dried parsley
Optional: 1/2 to 1 t. sugar
salt and pepper to taste
1 to 2 c. shredded Colby Jack or
  mild Cheddar cheese

Cook macaroni according to package directions, for shortest time recommended; drain. Meanwhile, in a large skillet over medium heat, brown beef with onion and garlic; drain. Add tomatoes with juice, tomato sauce and herbs to beef mixture; stir to mix. If tomatoes are too acidic, stir in sugar to taste. Add cooked macaroni to skillet; toss to mix well. Season with salt and pepper. Transfer mixture to a greased 13"x9" baking pan; top with cheese. Bake, uncovered, at 350 degrees for 20 minutes, or until bubbly and cheese is melted. Makes 10 servings.

December is jam-packed with shopping, decorating and baking, so take it easy with simple, hearty meals. Early in the holiday season, make double batches of family favorites like casseroles, chili or Sloppy Joes and freeze half to heat & eat later. You'll be so glad you did!

Sharing Christmas
Together

Baked Bowtie Pasta

Tiffany Jones
Batesville, AR

This pasta is so comforting and delicious! The bow-shaped pasta is fun for Christmastime, too.

12-oz. pkg. bowtie pasta,
  uncooked
15-oz. container ricotta cheese
8-oz. pkg. shredded Italian-blend
  cheese

3/4 c. grated Parmesan cheese
1 t. garlic powder
1 t. onion powder
salt and pepper to taste
24-oz. jar vodka pasta sauce

Cook pasta according to package directions; drain. Meanwhile, in a large bowl, combine remaining ingredients except pasta sauce. Add cooked pasta and mix well; transfer to a greased 3-quart casserole dish. Spoon pasta sauce over pasta mixture. Bake, uncovered, at 400 degrees for 20 minutes, or until hot and bubbly. Serves 6.

Cindy's Chicken Spaghetti

Marian Forck
Chamois, MO

My sister in law made this for a family function and it was a big hit! Everyone loved it and she had many ask for the recipe. She tripled the recipe and served in a big electric roaster.

8-oz. pkg. spaghetti, uncooked
10-3/4 oz. can cream of
  mushroom soup
10-oz. can diced tomatoes
  with green chiles

8-oz. container sour cream
2 c. grilled chicken, cubed
8-oz. pkg. shredded Mexican-
  blend cheese

Cook spaghetti according to package directions; drain and transfer to a large bowl. Add remaining ingredients except cheese; mix well. Transfer to a lightly greased 13"x9" baking pan. Cover with aluminum foil; bake at 350 degrees for 30 minutes. Sprinkle cheese on top and return to oven until cheese is melted. Serves 6 to 8.

Taking a casserole to a holiday potluck? Tie on a tag with the recipe name, made from a Christmas card.

Christmas
for Sharing

Slow-Cooker Pineapple Pork Loin
Shirley Howie
Foxboro, MA

With minimal prep time, this full-flavored, sweet and savory roast makes a great family weeknight dinner, yet is special enough to serve to guests.

2 to 3-lb. pork loin, fat trimmed
salt and pepper to taste
2 T. oil
4 cloves garlic, minced

20-oz. can pineapple chunks
1/4 c. soy sauce
1/2 c. brown sugar, packed

Season pork loin with salt and pepper; set aside. Heat oil in a large skillet over medium-high heat. Brown pork on each side for 2 to 4 minutes, until golden. Transfer to a 5-quart slow cooker; rub with garlic and set aside. In a bowl, combine pineapple chunks with juice and soy sauce. Spoon around pork in slow cooker. Sprinkle brown sugar evenly over pork. Cover and cook on low setting for 5 to 6 hours, until tender. Slice and serve, topped with pineapple mixture. Makes 6 servings.

Baked sweet potatoes are delicious with roast pork. Pierce potatoes several times with a fork, and put them right on the oven rack. At 325 degrees, they'll be tender in about one hour. Slice open and top with butter; sprinkle with cinnamon-sugar, or go for savory spices like cumin, paprika and garlic powder. It couldn't be easier!

Sharing Christmas
Together

Old-Fashioned Pot Roast

Diana Krol
Hutchinson, KS

This is our family favorite...comfort food deluxe, the perfect holiday dinner, Sunday lunch or a whole meal to carry to a friend. Your home will smell heavenly as it cooks!

2 onions, thinly sliced
1 c. water
1 bay leaf
3 to 4-lb. beef chuck roast
paprika, salt and pepper to taste

4 to 6 carrots, peeled and
  quartered
4 to 6 potatoes, peeled and
  quartered

Make a bed of sliced onions in the bottom of a roasting pan. Add water and bay leaf to pan; set aside. Season roast with paprika, salt and pepper; place roast on top of onions. Cover and bake at 325 degrees for 3 to 4 hours. After 1-1/2 hours, turn roast over; arrange vegetables around roast. Cover and continue baking until done. Discard bay leaf and serve. Makes 6 to 8 servings.

Set a pine-scented potted rosemary wreath in a kitchen window...so handy for adding flavorful fresh sprigs to roasting meats and vegetables.

Christmas
for Sharing

Chicken & Broccoli Casserole

Julia Bondi
Chicago, IL

I don't remember how long I have been making this recipe, I know
it is many years! We have never grown tired of it. This can be
made with any kind of cooked veggie in place of broccoli.

4 boneless, skinless chicken
    breasts
10-oz. pkg. frozen chopped
    broccoli
10-3/4 oz. can cream of
    chicken soup
1/2 c. mayonnaise

1 t. lemon juice
1/2 to 3/4 c. seasoned dry
    bread crumbs
1-1/2 to 2 c. shredded Cheddar
    cheese
cooked rice or egg noodles

In a large saucepan, cover chicken with water. Cook over medium heat
for about 15 minutes, until tender. Drain; cut into bite-size pieces and
set aside. Meanwhile, cook broccoli according to package directions;
drain and set aside. In a large bowl, mix together soup, mayonnaise and
lemon juice; fold in chicken and broccoli. Transfer to a lightly greased
2-quart casserole dish. Bake, uncovered, at 350 degrees for 30 minutes,
or until hot and bubbly. Top with bread crumbs and cheese; return to
oven and bake until cheese is melted. Serve with cooked rice or noodles.
Makes 4 servings.

For an easy side that goes well with casseroles, whip up
a marinated salad to keep in the fridge. Cut up crunchy
veggies and toss with zesty Italian salad dressing.

Sharing Christmas
Together

Mom & Dad's Party Chicken

Carolyn Tellers
Erie, PA

My mom & dad have fixed this recipe for years for company, usually during the fall or winter. Serve with steamed rice.

4-oz. pkg. chopped, pressed beef
8 boneless, skinless chicken
   breasts
8 slices bacon

10-3/4 oz. can cream of
   mushroom soup
1 c. sour cream

Spread beef in the bottom of a greased 13"x9" baking pan; set aside. Wrap each piece of chicken with a slice of bacon. Arrange chicken on top of beef. In a bowl, stir together soup and sour cream; spoon over chicken. Bake, uncovered, at 350 degrees for 45 minutes to one hour, until chicken is cooked through. Makes 8 servings.

Sweet-and-Sour Chicken

Leona Krivda
Belle Vernon, PA

There can never be too many recipes for chicken! We eat it often at our house, and I am always looking for new way to fix it. This is a great one!

4 boneless, skinless, chicken
   breasts
garlic powder, salt and pepper
   to taste

8-oz. bottle Russian salad
   dressing
10-oz. jar apricot preserves
1.35-oz. pkg. onion soup mix

Lightly sprinkle chicken breasts on both sides with seasonings. Arrange chicken in a well-buttered 13"x9" shallow baking pan; set aside. Whisk together remaining ingredients in a bowl; spoon over chicken. Bake, uncovered, at 350 degrees for 1-1/4 hours, spooning pan juices over chicken several times while baking. Serves 4.

Jazz up a packaged wild rice mix. Sauté a cup of chopped onion, celery and mushrooms in butter, then add rice mix and prepare as usual.

Christmas
for Sharing

Spaghetti Bake

Elisha Nelson
Brookline, MO

*This is a fun and easy recipe that the grown-ups and kids
will enjoy! Serve with some crusty bread and a crisp tossed salad.*

8-oz. pkg. spaghetti, uncooked
1/4 c. butter
2 t. olive oil
1 lb. ground beef
1 t. salt

1/2 t. pepper
32-oz. jar spaghetti sauce
8-oz. pkg. shredded mozzarella
   cheese
6-oz. pkg. sliced pepperoni

Cook spaghetti according to package directions; drain and transfer to a
large bowl. Add butter; toss to coat and set aside. Meanwhile, drizzle oil
in a large skillet over medium heat. Add beef and cook until browned;
drain. Season with salt and pepper. Stir in spaghetti sauce; simmer over
low heat for 3 to 5 minutes. Add half of beef mixture to spaghetti; gently
toss until well mixed. Transfer spaghetti mixture to an 8"x8" baking pan
coated with non-stick vegetable spray. Spread remaining beef mixture
over spaghetti. Sprinkle with cheese; arrange desired amount of
pepperoni over cheese. Cover with aluminum foil. Bake at 375 degrees
for 25 minutes. Remove foil; bake for additional 15 minutes, or until
hot and bubbly. Makes 4 to 6 servings.

Pull out all your favorite board games on a wintry day when
family & friends come to visit. Set out lots of tasty snacks
and turn up the Christmas music...terrific for all ages!

Sharing Christmas
Together

Slow-Cooker Short Ribs

Georgia Muth
Penn Valley, CA

This is a simple classic with comfort-food flavor. Short ribs are slow-cooked until they reach fall-off-the-bone deliciousness, freeing up your day for other activities. Serve with steamed rice or mashed potatoes, topped with the sauce from the slow cooker if desired.

3 to 4 lbs. boneless or bone-in
   beef short ribs
1 t. salt
1 t. pepper
1 to 2 T. oil

2 c. beef broth
1/4 c. Worcestershire sauce
1 t. garlic powder
1 t. onion powder
1 sprig fresh rosemary

Season short ribs with salt and pepper. Heat a large skillet over high heat; add oil. Brown short ribs on all 4 sides, about one minute per side. Meanwhile, in a 4-quart slow cooker, combine beef broth, Worcestershire sauce, garlic powder and onion powder; stir. Add short ribs to slow cooker; top with rosemary sprig. Cover and cook on low setting for 6 to 8 hours, until ribs are very tender. Discard rosemary before serving. Makes 4 to 6 servings.

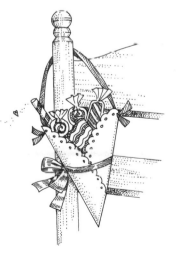

For a sweet welcome, fill Victorian-style paper cones
with old-fashioned hard candies and hang from
chair backs with ribbons.

Christmas
for Sharing

Chicken Stroganoff

Sherryll Wallace
Indianola, IA

My husband isn't fond of noodles, so I tweaked my beef stroganoff recipe using rice instead, and he just loved it! The sour cream chive dip really added that extra flavor it needed. Add a tossed salad and rolls or garlic bread and you have a warm, cozy, comfort meal for those cold, wintry days. Try different kinds of soup and sour cream dip to change the flavor, too.

1-1/4 lbs. boneless, skinless
   chicken breasts
1 c. long-cooking rice, uncooked
2 c. chicken broth
4 T. butter, divided
1/2 c. onion, chopped

salt and pepper to taste
10-3/4 oz. can cream of
   celery soup
8-oz. container sour cream
   chive dip
1-1/2 t. Worcestershire sauce

Cut chicken breasts into thin strips, about 1-1/2 inches long; set aside. In a large saucepan, combine rice, chicken broth and one tablespoon butter. Bring to a boil. Reduce heat; cover and simmer for 20 minutes, or until broth has been absorbed and rice is done; set aside. Meanwhile, melt 2 tablespoons butter in a large skillet over medium-high heat. Add onion; cook for 10 minutes, or until caramelized and golden. Add remaining butter, chicken, salt and pepper to skillet. Cook, stirring often, until chicken is cooked through. Add remaining ingredients; stir until well blended. Bring to a gentle simmer over low heat. If mixture seems too thick, stir in a little milk or water to desired consistency. Divide cooked rice among 4 dinner plates; top with chicken mixture. Serves 4.

For somehow, not only at Christmas,
But all the year through,
The joy that you give to others
Is the joy that comes back to you.

–Margaret Sangster

Sharing Christmas
Together

Cheesy Smoky Potato Bake

Laura Witham
Anchorage, AK

One wintry Alaska night, I was looking for something to serve my family. I didn't want to brave the winter chill just for a few ingredients, so I made a dish out of what I had on hand. The result was scrumptious...and it tasted even better the next day!

14-oz. pkg. Kielbasa or other
    smoked pork sausage, diced
1 T. extra-virgin olive oil
1 onion, diced
2 cloves garlic, minced
salt and pepper to taste
2-1/2 lbs. redskin potatoes,
    cubed

1-1/2 c. chicken broth
10-3/4 oz. can cream of
    chicken soup
1/2 c. mayonnaise
1/2 c. milk
8-oz. pkg. shredded Cheddar
    cheese, divided

In a skillet over medium-high heat, sauté sausage in olive oil for 3 to 5 minutes, until fat begins to render. Reduce heat to medium. Add onion, garlic, salt and pepper. Sauté for about 3 minutes, until onion becomes translucent. Add potatoes; sauté for one minute. Add chicken broth and bring to a boil. Cook, stirring often, until most of broth has cooked out. Remove from heat. In a saucepan over medium heat, stir together soup, mayonnaise and milk; bring to a low simmer. Add half of cheese and stir until melted. Spoon cheese mixture over sausage mixture; stir well. Transfer to a lightly greased 13"x9" baking pan; sprinkle with remaining cheese. Cover with aluminum foil. Bake at 350 degrees for 45 to 50 minutes, until potatoes are tender. Remove from oven. Let stand for 10 minutes, or until cooled and thickened; serve. Makes 6 to 8 servings.

Giving a large, hard-to-wrap gift this year? Hide it! Wrap up a smaller gift...for example, a bicycle bell for a new bike or a little doll for a doll house. Tie on a gift tag hinting at where to look for the large gift. Half the work and twice the fun!

Christmas
for Sharing

Slow-Cooker All-Day Cassoulet

Bev Traxler
British Columbia, Canada

When my grandkids pay a visit, this is the first meal they sit down to! I have done it this way for nearly 30 years...it's a tried & true recipe. You can vary the type of beans you use.

1-1/2 lbs. smoked Polish pork
    sausage, sliced 1/4-inch thick
3 c. shredded Cheddar cheese
2 15-oz. cans pork & beans
2 15-oz. cans kidney beans
15-oz. can lima beans, drained
10-3/4 oz. can tomato soup
3/4 c. onion, chopped

1/2 c. green pepper, chopped
1/4 c. golden syrup or light
    corn syrup
1/2 t. dry mustard
1/2 t. pepper
Garnish: additional shredded
    cheese, sliced green onions

In a 6-quart slow cooker, combine all ingredients except garnish; mix well. Cover and cook on low setting for 8 to 10 hours, until hot and bubbly. Garnish servings with additional cheese and green onions, as desired. Makes 10 servings.

Start a new family tradition...call everyone in to dinner by ringing a dinner bell! You can even let the kids take turns ringing the bell on different nights.

Sharing Christmas
Together

Mom's Glazed Holiday Ham

Paula Marchesi
Auburn, PA

Every Christmas, I'm asked to prepare this delicious ham, and I'm always happy to oblige because it's so easy to prepare. I've been making this for over 25 years now! If there are any leftovers, they make delicious sandwiches.

7 to 9-lb. spiral-sliced fully
    cooked bone-in ham
1/2 c. sugar
1/2 c. unsweetened applesauce
1/4 c. unsweetened apple juice
1/4 c. cranberry juice

1/4 c. pure maple syrup
1/4 c. molasses
1 T. Dijon mustard
1/8 t. cinnamon
1/8 t. ground ginger

Place ham in an ungreased shallow roasting pan. Bake, uncovered, at 325 degrees for 2 hours. Meanwhile, in a small saucepan over medium heat, combine remaining ingredients. Cook and stir until heated through and sugar is dissolved. After ham has baked for 2 hours, brush with some of the glaze. Bake, uncovered, at 325 degrees for 40 to 60 minutes longer, or until a meat thermometer inserted in the thickest part reads 140 degrees; brush occasionally with remaining glaze. Remove from oven; let stand 4 to 5 minutes before serving. Serves 15.

Keep the Christmas dinner menu simple, familiar and yummy. You may even want to ask your family ahead of time what dishes or foods are "special" to them. It's a day for tradition and comfort...and you'll be a more relaxed hostess too.

161

Christmas
for Sharing

Hearty Sausage & Cabbage Skillet   *Sacha George*
Kalamazoo, MI

This hearty skillet meal is delicious on a winter evening here in Michigan! It is also simple to make. Perfect for a cold night after a long, busy day. Add a can of red beans, if that sounds good to you. Serve with warm cornbread.

2 T. butter
1 T. olive oil
2 potatoes, peeled and cut into
    bite-size cubes
1 onion, diced
1 to 2 t. garlic, minced
salt and pepper to taste
1 head green cabbage, chopped

14-1/2 oz. can sliced carrots,
    drained
1 T. white vinegar
1/4 c. chicken broth, or more
    as needed
14-oz. pkg. Polska Kielbasa
    turkey sausage, cut into
    bite-size slices

In an electric skillet or stovetop skillet over medium heat, melt butter with oil. Add potatoes, onion, garlic, salt and pepper; sauté over medium-high heat until softened. Add cabbage; cook for one to 2 minutes. Add carrots, vinegar, chicken broth and sausage. Simmer for 10 minutes, or until all ingredients are cooked through. Makes 8 servings.

Do you love cabbage and sauerkraut for winter meals, but hate the smell? Here's Grandma's little trick. Lay a slice of bread on top before covering the pot, and there will be no cabbage aroma. Afterwards, just toss out the bread.

Sharing Christmas
Together

Tasty Pork Chops

Estelle Hugger
Sugarloaf, PA

*When these pork chops are simmering in the slow cooker,
the whole house smells like someone's been cooking bacon!*

4 to 6 pork chops, 1-inch thick
10-3/4 oz. can cream of
   mushroom soup
8-oz. container sour cream

4-oz. can sliced mushrooms,
   drained
1 T. Worcestershire sauce
salt and pepper to taste

Layer pork chops in a 5-quart slow cooker; set aside. Combine remaining ingredients in a bowl; mix well and spoon over pork chops. Cover and cook on low setting for 7 to 8 hours, until pork chops are cooked through. Serve pork chops topped with mushrooms and sauce from crock. Makes 4 to 6 servings.

Easy Pork Chops

Patricia Nau
River Grove, IL

*My family loves this recipe for pork chops...they are always
tender and delicious. Mashed potatoes or steamed rice and
a fresh vegetable complete this easy meal.*

2 T. olive oil
6 boneless pork chops,
   1-inch thick
paprika, kosher salt and pepper
   to taste

2 yellow onions, thinly sliced and
   separated into rings
2 10-3/4 oz. cans chicken &
   rice soup

Heat oil in a large non-stick skillet over medium heat. Sprinkle pork chops with seasonings; add to skillet and brown on both sides. Cover pork chops with all of the onion rings; spoon chicken soup over onions. Reduce heat to medium-low; cover and simmer for 30 minutes. Turn pork chops over. Cover and continue to cook for a few more minutes, until pork chops are done. Serve pork chops topped with onions and pan juices. Makes 6 servings.

Christmas
for Sharing

Shrimp & Pasta in Lemon-Garlic Sauce

Michelle Papp
Rutherford, NJ

Easy enough for weeknights, yet good for company too.
You'll love the savory sauce.

9-oz. pkg. refrigerated linguine
    pasta, uncooked
2 T. olive oil
1/4 c. butter
4 cloves garlic, minced
1 c. chicken broth, or more
    as needed

zest of 1 lemon
juice of 1/2 lemon
12 to 16 cooked extra-large
    shrimp, peeled
salt and pepper to taste
3 T. fresh parsley, chopped

Cook pasta according to package directions; drain. Meanwhile, heat olive oil in a large skillet over medium heat. Add butter and garlic; cook for 3 to 4 minutes. Add chicken broth, lemon zest and juice to skillet; cook for about 10 minutes. Add shrimp and cooked pasta to skillet; toss to coat and heat through. Add a little more broth, if a lighter sauce is desired. Season with salt and pepper; sprinkle with parsley and serve. Makes 4 servings.

For a special touch when serving seafood, wrap lemon halves in cheesecloth, tie with a colorful ribbon and set one on each plate. The cheesecloth prevents squirting and catches any seeds.

Sharing Christmas
Together

Lisa's Crabby Cakes

Lisa Ann Panzino DiNunzio
Vineland, NJ

These crab cakes are moist, flavorful and simply delicious!
Serve them on your favorite sandwich buns, or on a bed of
lettuce with several lemon wedges on the side.

1 lb. fresh lump crabmeat, flaked
2/3 c. Italian-seasoned dry
   bread crumbs
1/4 c. mayonnaise
1 T. mustard
1 egg, beaten

1 T. lemon juice
1 T. fresh parsley, finely chopped
1 t. seafood seasoning
salt and pepper to taste
2 T. butter, melted

In a large bowl, combine all ingredients except butter. Gently fold together with a rubber spatula. Form mixture into 6 patties; place on a parchment paper-lined rimmed baking sheet. Brush tops with melted butter. Bake at 450 degrees for 25 to 30 minutes, until a meat thermometer inserted in the center reads 165 degrees. Makes 6 servings.

Mix up a quick homemade sauce for crab cakes and other fish dishes. Combine 1/4 cup tartar sauce, 1-1/2 tablespoons lemon juice, one teaspoon seafood seasoning and 1/2 teaspoon Worcestershire sauce. Chill until serving time.

Egg Roll Noodle Bowl

Courtney Stultz
Weir, KS

We love egg rolls, but they can be a lot of fuss to make. We decided to simplify the idea and turn it into a skillet dish, served in bowls! The meal still has great flavor and is loaded with veggies. Serve with crispy fried wontons for a little crunch.

1/2 lb. ground pork, beef
   or chicken
1 T. sesame oil
1 small head cabbage, sliced
2 carrots, peeled and grated
3 green onions, diced
1/2 t. garlic, minced
1 T. soy sauce

1 t. ground ginger
1/4 t. turmeric
1/2 t. sea salt
1/2 t. pepper
1 to 2 c. rice noodles or angel
   hair pasta, uncooked
Garnish: sliced green onions

In a large skillet over medium heat, brown meat in oil; drain. Stir in cabbage, carrots, onions, garlic, soy sauce and seasonings. Cook over medium heat for about 10 more minutes, stirring often, until vegetables are cooked. Meanwhile, cook noodles or pasta according to package directions. Drain and add to skillet; mix gently. Serve topped with green onions. Serves 4.

If your family has a tradition of going out at Christmas for Chinese food, why not enjoy it at home? Stir up an easy recipe to serve with steamed rice or rice noodles. For dessert, scoop sherbet into stemmed glasses, then slip a fortune cookie over the edge of each glass.

Sharing Christmas
Together

Pork Chop Suey

Sharry Murawski
Oak Forest, IL

This recipe makes a large pot! We always plan on leftovers for another meal...it also freezes well. You can substitute beef stew meat in place of the pork.

1/2 c. all-purpose flour
2 t. salt
2 lbs. boneless pork, cubed
2 to 3 T. oil
2 c. onion, chopped
2 c. celery, chopped
15-oz. can baby corn cobs, drained
2 8-oz. cans sliced water chestnuts, drained
8-oz. can sliced mushrooms, drained
2 c. beef broth
1 c. low-sodium soy sauce
1/4 c. molasses
28-oz. can bean sprouts, drained
Optional: 1 to 2 T. all-purpose flour or cornstarch, cold water
cooked rice

Combine flour and salt in a shallow dish. Add pork cubes; toss to coat. Heat oil in a large Dutch oven over medium heat. Working in batches, add pork cubes and cook until browned. Add onion and cook until golden. Stir in celery, corn cobs, water chestnuts, mushrooms, beef broth, soy sauce and molasses. Bring to boil. Reduce heat to medium-low; cover and simmer for 30 minutes. Add bean sprouts; simmer for 15 minutes more. If a thicker consistency is desired, mix flour or cornstarch with just enough cold water to make a liquid mixture. Stir into mixture in pan; bring to a boil and cook until thickened. Serve over cooked rice. Makes 8 generous servings.

Place newly arrived Christmas cards in a vintage napkin holder, then take a moment every evening to share happy holiday greetings from friends & neighbors over dinner.

Christmas
for Sharing

Roast Pork with Raspberry
Balsamic Pan Sauce

Jackie Bakunas
Forest Hill, MD

When you want to make something that's simple, yet impressive, this is the perfect recipe! It sounds fancy, looks fancy, yet is oh-so easy to make. My whole family gets excited when I make this for dinner, even our young kids! For a delicious, juicy roast, check the the center with a meat thermometer and don't let it get over 140 degrees.

2-1/2 lb. pork loin roast
fine sea salt and pepper to taste
2 T. butter
2 T. olive oil
14-1/2 oz. can chicken broth
1 shallot, minced

4 cloves garlic, minced
1/4 c. balsamic vinegar
18-oz. jar raspberry preserves
1 t. Dijon mustard
1 t. dried rosemary

Season roast generously on all sides with salt and pepper. Heat a deep skillet over high heat until sizzling hot; melt butter with olive oil. Add roast and brown on all sides, about 5 minutes per side. Set a wire rack in a roasting pan; add chicken broth to pan. Add roast to pan, fat-side up; set aside skillet, reserving drippings. Bake, uncovered, at 350 degrees for 25 minutes (about 10 minutes per pound), or to desired doneness. A meat thermometer inserted in the thickest part of roast will measure 135 to 140 degrees for medium-rare. Remove from oven; cover loosely and let stand for 10 minutes. Meanwhile, add shallot to reserved drippings in skillet. Cook over medium heat for one minute. Add garlic; cook for one minute. Add vinegar; continue cooking for one minute while using a wooden spoon to scrape and loosen pan drippings in bottom of skillet. Reduce heat to low; stir in preserves, mustard and rosemary. Continue to cook over low heat for about 10 minutes, stirring often. Season with additional salt and pepper, if desired. Slice roast and serve with pan sauce. Serves 4.

An easy side dish...quarter new potatoes and toss with a little
olive oil, salt and pepper. Spread in a baking pan and bake
at 350 degrees for about one hour, until crisp and golden.

Sharing Christmas
Together

Mom's Melt-in-Your-Mouth Pork Chops

Pat Martin
Riverside, CA

My mother taught me how to make these tender pork chops many years ago. They are the best I've ever tasted...true comfort food! If chops are greater than one inch thick, slice them horizontally.

3 to 4 eggs
1 to 2 c. all-purpose flour
1 to 2 t. salt
1 to 2 t. pepper
1 to 2 c. buttery round crackers
    or saltine crackers, finely
    crushed

6 to 8 boneless pork chops,
    one inch thick
1/4 to 1/2 c. canola oil
1 to 2 c. hot water

Beat eggs in a shallow dish. Spread flour on a plate; mix in salt and pepper. Spread cracker crumbs in another shallow dish. Dip pork chops into egg mixture, then into flour, again into egg, then into crackers. Heat oil in a large skillet over medium-high heat. Working in batches as needed, brown pork chops on both sides, removing to a plate when done. Return all browned chops to the skillet, overlapping slightly as necessary. Carefully pour hot water around chops. Cover and simmer over very low heat for 1- 1/2 to 2 hours, depending on thickness of chops. Makes 6 to 8 servings.

Invite friends to join you for a favorite skillet or slow-cooker supper in December...a meal shared with friends doesn't need to be fancy. After all, it's friendship that makes it special!

Christmas
for Sharing

Porcupine Meatballs

Marilyn Roberts
Alamo, TN

This is a recipe my grandmother would make for holidays.
We called it Maw Maw Meatballs, and everyone loved them.

1-1/2 lbs. ground beef
1 c. long-cooking rice, uncooked
1/2 c. onion, chopped
1 egg, beaten
1/4 t. garlic powder
salt to taste

1/8 t. pepper
2 10-3/4 oz. cans cream of
   chicken soup
10-3/4 oz. can cream of
   mushroom soup
1 c. water

In a large bowl, combine all ingredients except soups and water. Mix well and form into walnut-size balls. Place meatballs in a Dutch oven; set aside. Whisk together soups and water in another bowl; spoon over meatballs. Cover and bake at 350 degrees for 45 minutes. Uncover and bake 15 more minutes. To use a slow cooker, cover and cook on high setting for 4 to 5 hours, or on low setting for 6 to 7 hours. Serves 8.

The crackle of a warm, cozy fire on a winter day brings
everyone together. Enjoy a simple dinner of roasted hot dogs
or toasty pie-iron sandwiches, then make s'mores together
and enjoy mugs of warm spiced cider.

Sharing Christmas
Together

Taco Taters

Carolyn Deckard
Bedford, IN

My kids, grandkids and now great-grandkids enjoy this recipe...especially on a snow day off from school!

6 russet potatoes
1 lb. ground beef
1-1/4 oz. pkg. taco
   seasoning mix

24-oz. jar favorite pasta sauce
Optional: shredded Cheddar
   cheese, sour cream

Pierce potatoes with a fork. Bake at 425 degrees for one hour, or until fork-tender. Meanwhile, brown beef in a skillet over medium-high heat; drain. Stir in taco seasoning and pasta sauce; simmer for 5 to 10 minutes. To serve, cut a lengthwise slice from top of each potato. Evenly spoon beef mixture onto each potato. Garnish as desired. Makes 6 servings.

Betty's Potato Topping

Tamela James
Grove City, OH

My mother-in-law has been making this recipe since she was a young girl. We also make barbecue beef, broccoli and cheese baked potatoes and this is delicious on those as well. We even bake a few extra potatoes to enjoy later. Everyone loves it!

1 c. butter, softened
16-oz. container sour cream
8-oz. pkg. shredded Cheddar
   cheese

garlic salt to taste
russet potatoes, baked
   and split

In a large bowl, mix butter and sour cream well. Add cheese and garlic salt; mix well. Cover and refrigerate until serving time. Makes enough for 16 baked potatoes.

Variation: Slice baked potatoes; brown on each side in a skillet. Add a dollop of topping to each slice and serve.

Christmas
for Sharing

Mother's Manicotti

KellyJean Gettelfinger
Sellersburg, IN

This recipe was passed on to me from my husband's mother. I had never eaten a manicotti dish until I met my husband. Since we've been married, I have tried all sorts of manicotti meals, but none of them are like my mother-in-law's. I treasure this recipe! I have her recipe card for this dish in her own handwriting, and I treasure it just as much than the recipe itself. Maybe more!

8-oz. pkg. manicotti shells,
    uncooked
3/4 c. onion, finely chopped
3/4 c. green pepper,
    finely chopped
1 stalk celery, finely chopped
4 cloves garlic, minced
1/4 c. olive oil
1/2 lb. ground beef
1/2 lb. ground pork
10-oz. pkg. frozen chopped
    spinach, thawed and drained

1 c. grated Parmesan cheese
1/2 c. fresh parsley, chopped
2 eggs, well beaten
1/2 c. Italian-seasoned dry
    bread crumbs
1-1/2 t. dried oregano
1 t. salt
1 t. pepper
3 to 4 8-oz. cans tomato sauce
Optional: additional grated
    Parmesan cheese

Cook manicotti according to package directions; drain. Meanwhile, in a large skillet over medium heat, sauté onion, green pepper, celery and garlic in olive oil. Add meats and brown; drain well. Stir in spinach, cheese, parsley and eggs. Simmer over low heat until well blended and browned. Stir in bread crumbs and seasonings; cook until firm. Spoon meat mixture into manicotti shells; arrange side by side in a lightly greased 13"x9" shallow baking pan. Cover shells with tomato sauce. Bake, uncovered, at 350 degrees for 40 to 45 minutes. Serve with additional Parmesan cheese as desired. Serves 8 to 12.

Keep a chunk of Parmesan cheese fresh longer...wrap it in a paper towel moistened with cider vinegar, tuck it into a plastic zipping bag and refrigerate.

Sharing Christmas
Together

Italian Meat Sauce

Jane Granger
Manteno, IL

This recipe was my mother Margaret's recipe. Enjoy it over your favorite pasta, with some hot garlic bread on the side.

1 lb. ground beef	1/4 t. celery flakes
14-1/2 oz. can diced tomatoes	1/4 t. dried oregano
6-oz. can tomato paste	1/4 t. dried basil
2 c. water	1/2 t. dried parsley
1 T. butter	1 t. salt
1 clove garlic, chopped	1/4 t. pepper
1/2 t. dried, minced onions	1 bay leaf

Brown beef in a large skillet over medium heat; drain. Add tomatoes with juice and remaining ingredients; mix well. Simmer over medium-low heat for one hour, or until thickened, stirring occasionally. Discard bay leaf before serving. Makes 4 servings.

When family members are visiting for the holidays, be sure to get out the old picture albums, slides and family films. What a joy to reminisce together, laugh and share special memories of childhood and Christmases past!

Christmas
for Sharing

Cranberry Salmon with Wild Rice Pilaf

Katie Wollgast
Troy, MO

I love salmon for its flavor and fast cooking time. I also love to serve elegant holiday meals. Some of my favorites are dishes with cranberry sauces or gravies. I thought, why not try it with salmon? And, here is the result! I often make a homemade pilaf, but using a favorite boxed mix works to keep it simple. Easily double or triple the recipe for more guests.

6-oz. pkg. long-grain & wild
   rice mix
1/2 t. dried thyme
1/2 t. salt
1/4 t. pepper
4 4-oz. skinless salmon fillets
2 to 3 t. oil
1/2 c. whole-berry cranberry
   sauce
1 t. Worcestershire sauce
1 t. soy sauce

1 t. lemon juice
1 T. cornstarch
1/2 c. cranberry juice cocktail
   or water
1/2 c. frozen green peas
Garnish: 1/4 c. plain yogurt,
   1/4 c. grated Parmesan
   cheese
Optional: chopped green onions,
   dried cranberries, sliced
   almonds

Cook rice mix according to package instructions. Meanwhile, combine seasonings and rub over skinless side of salmon fillets. Heat oil in a skillet over medium heat; add salmon, seasoned side down. Cook until browned; carefully turn salmon over. In a bowl, whisk together all sauces and lemon juice; add to skillet and bring to a boil. Whisk together cornstarch and juice or water in same bowl; add to skillet. Reduce heat to low; cook and gently stir sauce until thickened. Cover and simmer for 5 minutes, or until salmon flakes easily with a fork. Stir peas into rice mixture; fluff with a fork. Serve salmon beside or over the pilaf, spooning cranberry pan sauce over each fillet. Top each serving with a dollop of yogurt and sprinkle with cheese; sprinkle with onions, cranberries and almonds, if desired. Serves 4.

A merry Christmas to everybody!
A happy New Year to all the world!
–Charles Dickens

Sharing Christmas
Together

Linguine with Red Clam Sauce

Mia Rossi
Charleston, SC

As an Italian family, we always have seafood dishes on Christmas Eve. This one is quick, easy and delicious.

12-oz. pkg. linguine pasta,
  uncooked
2 t. olive oil
2 t. garlic, minced
24-oz. jar marinara pasta sauce

2 T. sun-dried or regular
  tomato paste
1/4 t. red pepper flakes
3 6-1/2 oz. cans chopped clams,
  drained and juice reserved

Cook pasta according to package directions; drain. Meanwhile, heat oil in a saucepan over medium heat. Add garlic and sauté for 2 minutes. Stir in marinara sauce, tomato paste and red pepper flakes; bring to a simmer. Stir reserved clam juice into sauce mixture; simmer for 10 minutes. Stir in clams and simmer for 3 minutes. Serve pasta with sauce. Makes 6 servings.

Lemon Butter Scallops

Vickie
Gooseberry Patch

Oh-so easy and delicious! Serve with steamed rice.

1 lb. large scallops
salt and pepper to taste
1 T. canola oil
2 T. butter

1 clove garlic, minced
1/4 c. lemon juice
2 T. fresh parsley, snipped

Pat scallops dry with a paper towel; season with salt and pepper. Heat oil in a skillet over medium-high heat until very hot. Add scallops; cook on each side for 2 to 4 minutes, until golden and not quite cooked through. Transfer scallops to a bowl; set aside. Melt butter in skillet. Add garlic and cook for about 30 seconds, until fragrant. Stir in lemon juice and parsley; drizzle butter mixture over scallops and serve. Makes 4 servings.

Christmas
for Sharing

Oh-So-Easy Roast Chicken

Jo Ann
Gooseberry Patch

Sheet-pan easy for the holidays! Choose everyone's fave pieces of chicken. Serving a crowd? Just fill a second pan and bake at the same time, swapping sheet pans in the oven halfway through baking time.

3 T. olive oil
2 T. soy sauce
2 T. red wine vinegar
1 T. light brown sugar, packed
4 shallots, chopped

2 cloves garlic, minced
6 to 8 chicken thighs
   and/or breasts
salt and pepper to taste

In a small bowl, combine olive oil, soy sauce, vinegar, brown sugar, shallots and garlic. Mix well; spread over a large rimmed baking sheet. Add chicken pieces to pan; toss to coat well and season generously with salt and pepper. Turn chicken pieces skin-side up. Bake at 425 degrees for 30 minutes, or until chicken begins to turn golden. Turn chicken over; spoon pan juices over chicken. Bake another 10 minutes, or until chicken juices run clear when pierced. Serves 4 to 6.

If the kids are always too excited on Christmas Day to sit down for a formal dinner, set out a make-ahead buffet of sliced baked ham or roast turkey, rolls or bread. Add a favorite side dish warming in a slow cooker, and for dessert, a platter of Christmas cookies. Relax...you'll enjoy the day more, too!

Sharing Christmas
Together

Poor Man's Prime Rib

Beth Ann Richter
Canby, MN

The secret to this recipe is in the seasoning. Once you try it, you'll never go back to making your roast the "regular" way again. I prefer chuck roast, but any cut will work as long as it doesn't have a lot of gristle. Enjoy!

3-lb. beef chuck roast
1 t. seasoning salt

1 t. onion salt
1/2 t. garlic powder

Preheat oven to 500 degrees. Season roast as desired; place roast in a roasting pan. Do not cover or add any water. Place roast in preheated oven; turn oven to 475 degrees. Bake for 21 minutes (about 7 minutes per pound). Turn oven off; leave roast in hot oven for 2-1/2 hours. Do not open oven door at all during this time! Remove roast from oven; a meat thermometer inserted in the center should read at least 145 degrees. Remove to a serving platter; let stand for several minutes and slice thinly. Makes 6 to 10 servings.

Mum's Yorkshire Pudding

Debra Hutchinson
Franklin, IN

I grew up eating Yorkshire pudding with roast beef. My mum, a World War II bride from England, made this for our Sunday dinner. Now I fix it for my sister, who is happy for our memory of Mum's Sunday dinners.

1/2 c. roast beef pan drippings
3/4 c. all-purpose flour
1/2 t. salt

3 eggs, beaten
3/4 c. milk

Pour drippings into a 9" pie plate or cast-iron skillet. Place pan in oven set to 450 degrees and heat through. Meanwhile, combine flour and salt in a bowl. In another bowl, beat together eggs and milk until light and foamy; stir in flour mixture. Carefully remove hot pan from oven; pour in batter. Bake at 450 degrees for 15 to 20 minutes, until puffed and dry. Cut into squares and serve. Serves 6.

Christmas
for Sharing

Oven-Baked Honey-Mustard Chicken

Shirley Howie
Foxboro, MA

This is a great no-fuss weeknight dinner that comes together in a jiffy! The honey-mustard sauce, combined with the chicken juices, is so flavorful and yummy! Sometimes I substitute basil or thyme for the oregano and it is equally delicious.

2 lbs. boneless, skinless
    chicken thighs
1/4 c. Dijon mustard
1/4 c. honey
1 T. olive oil

1/2 t. salt
1/4 t. pepper
1/2 t. dried oregano
1/8 t. cayenne pepper

Arrange chicken thighs in a lightly greased 13"x9" baking pan; set aside. In a small bowl, combine remaining ingredients; mix well. Spoon sauce over chicken, coating evenly. Bake, uncovered, at 350 degrees for 40 to 45 minutes, until the top is golden and juices run clear when chicken is pierced. Serves 4 to 6.

Chalkboard pots...clever holders for gifts of herb plants or serving bread sticks on the dinner table. Simply paint terra-cotta flowerpots with chalkboard paint, then write a holiday greeting on them.

Sharing Christmas
Together

Beef & Mushroom Dijon

Roberta Simpkins
Mentor on the Lake, OH

You can also make this recipe in a Dutch oven.

2 T. oil, divided
1 lb. beef sirloin steak, cut into
   3/4-inch strips or cubes
   and divided
2 c. sliced mushrooms
1/2 c. onion, diced

10-3/4 oz. can cream of
   mushroom soup
1/2 c. water
2 T. Dijon mustard
2 T. dried parsley
cooked rice

Heat one tablespoon oil in a skillet over medium-high heat. Add half of beef; brown on all sides, stirring often. Remove browned beef to a plate; set aside. Repeat with remaining beef. Reduce heat to medium; add remaining oil, mushrooms and onion. Cook until tender. Stir in remaining ingredients except rice; bring to a boil. Return beef to skillet; stir in and heat through. Serve mixture over cooked rice. Makes 4 to 6 servings.

Setting a children's table for Christmas dinner? Make it playful!
Cover the tabletop with giftwrap, decorate paper cups and napkins
with holiday stickers and add a gingerbread house centerpiece.
The kids will beg to sit there!

Christmas
for Sharing

Brats & Kraut Supper

Janet Ambruster
Apex, NC

This is a great meal for all of us who eat sauerkraut for good luck on New Year's Day! Pop everything in the slow cooker and you'll be free to watch parades and football on television, or simply relax.

14-oz. can sauerkraut, drained
   and rinsed
2 to 3 redskin potatoes,
   thinly sliced
1 tart apple, cored and
   thickly sliced
1/2 c. onion, chopped
3/4 c. water

2 T. brown sugar, packed
1 t. chicken bouillon powder
1 t. caraway seed
1 clove garlic, minced
1 bay leaf
14-oz. Kielbasa sausage, cut into
   2-inch chunks

In a 5-quart slow cooker, combine all ingredients except Kielbasa. Mix gently; place Kielbasa on top. Cover and cook on high setting for 4 to 5 hours, until potatoes are fork-tender. Discard bay leaf and serve. Makes 6 servings.

On New Year's Eve, celebrate early with little ones who won't make it til midnight. Get out those party hats and noisemakers, and toast with sparkling white grape juice!

Sharing Christmas
Together

Jill's Hoppin' John

Jill Luffman
Mount Juliet, TN

I changed a few things in this traditional New Year's Day recipe to make it my own. Instead of adding the rice to the dish, you can serve it spooned over rice, if you prefer.

14-oz. pkg. Kielbasa turkey
    sausage, sliced 1/4-inch thick
14-1/2 oz. can chicken broth
1-1/2 c. cooked rice

2 15-oz. cans black-eyed
    peas, drained
2 c. fresh baby spinach

In a large saucepan over medium heat, cook Kielbasa in chicken broth for 5 to 10 minutes. Add remaining ingredients except spinach; simmer for 10 to 15 minutes. Stir in spinach during last 5 minutes; cook until wilted and serve. Makes 6 servings.

Crazy Crust Pizza Bake

Kara Kimerline
Galion, OH

This tasty recipe was shared with me by my mother-in-law Carol, who has since passed away It is very easy and fun to make with a variety of toppings...even customize it for each family member, if you like!

1 lb. ground beef
2 eggs, beaten
2/3 c. milk
1 c. all-purpose flour
1 t. Italian seasoning
salt and pepper to taste

Garnish: sliced pepperoni,
    onions, black olives,
    banana peppers
14-oz. jar pizza sauce
8-oz. pkg. shredded mozzarella
    cheese

Brown beef in a skillet over medium heat; drain and set aside. In a small bowl, beat eggs, milk, flour and seasonings until smooth. Pour batter into a greased 13"x9" baking pan; spoon beef and desired toppings over batter. Bake, uncovered, at 425 degrees for 25 to 30 minutes. Remove from oven. Top with pizza sauce and cheese; bake an additional 10 to 15 minutes. Let cool for 5 minutes; cut into squares and serve. Makes 6 to 8 servings.

Christmas
for Sharing

Mom's Creamy Macaroni Shells

Robin Younkin
Monterey, CA

My mother used to make this for us once a week. Some of my earliest memories are of holding the wooden spoon and stirring as quickly as I could while the cheese melted.

8-oz. pkg. small macaroni
    shells, uncooked
8-oz. pkg. shredded Cheddar
    cheese

8-oz. can tomato sauce
1/2 t. garlic salt
1/4 t. chili powder
salt and pepper to taste

Cook macaroni according to package directions. Drain and return to pan. Add cheese, stirring constantly over medium heat. Add tomato sauce and seasonings. Cook and stir until saucy and cheese is melted. Makes 8 servings.

For a charming centerpiece, fill a large, clear glass container half-full with fresh cranberries. Set a tall pillar candle in the center of the berries and tuck in holly and greens around the base.

Festive
Sweets & Treats

Gingerbread Dessert

Margie Bush
Peoria, IL

Our family always went to church on Christmas Eve,
and then came home to this gingerbread dessert.
It was such a delicious tradition!

1/2 c. butter	1/2 t. salt
1/2 c. sugar	1 t. cinnamon
1 egg, beaten	1 t. ground ginger
1 c. mild-flavored molasses	1/2 t. ground cloves
2-1/2 c. all-purpose flour	1 c. hot water
1-1/2 t. baking soda	Garnish: whipped cream

In a large bowl, blend together butter and sugar; beat in egg. Stir in molasses; set aside. In a separate bowl, sift together flour, baking soda, salt and spices. Blend flour mixture into butter mixture; stir in hot water. Pour batter into a greased 9" round cake pan. Bake at 350 degrees for about one hour, checking the center for doneness with a toothpick. Cut into wedges; serve topped with whipped cream. Makes 8 servings.

Create a holiday recipe scrapbook! Invite family members to share tried & true favorites, and make enough copies for everybody. Punch a hole in one corner and tie them together with a shiny ribbon. A gift idea everyone will love!

Festive
Sweets & Treats

Pumpkin Crunch Cake

Laura Malecha
Lonsdale, MN

This is our favorite dessert for holidays! It's so easy,
and delicious topped with a dollop of whipped cream.

15-oz. can pumpkin
12-oz. can evaporated milk
3 eggs, beaten
1-1/2 c. sugar
1 t. cinnamon

1/2 t. salt
18-1/2 oz. pkg. yellow cake mix
1-1/2 c. chopped pecans
1 c. butter, melted

Grease the bottom of a 13"x9" baking pan; set aside. In a bowl, stir
together pumpkin, evaporated milk, eggs, sugar, cinnamon and salt.
Pour batter into pan. Sprinkle batter with dry cake mix and pecans;
drizzle melted butter over pecans. Bake at 350 degrees for 50 to
55 minutes. Cut into squares. Makes 10 to 12 servings.

Rocky Road Squares

Glenna Kennedy
Ontario, Canada

My mom found or created this recipe more than 50 years ago. My kids
loved it, my husband loved it, everyone I know that has tasted it, loves
it. When I take it to work as a treat now and then, the pan always
comes home empty!

8-oz. pkg. semi-sweet
  chocolate chips
8-oz. pkg. butterscotch chips
1 egg, beaten
1/2 c. butter, sliced

1 c. icing sugar or powdered
  sugar
10-oz. pkg. pastel or white
  mini marshmallows
2/3 c. flaked coconut

In a saucepan over low heat, combine chocolate and butterscotch chips,
egg, butter and sugar. Cook and stir until chips are melted and smooth.
Remove from heat; let cool for 2 to 3 minutes, no longer. Quickly add
marshmallows; stir to coat well. Pour into a buttered 9"x9" baking pan;
sprinkle with coconut. Refrigerate until set; cut into squares with a
sharp knife. Makes 2 dozen.

Christmas
for Sharing

Cranberry Christmas Delights

Jennifer Day
Cresson, TX

These cookies are so soft and flavorful...my husband and kids just love them! I love to add a holiday touch when I bake in the winter, and cranberries are a perfect addition.

1-1/4 c. sugar
1-1/4 c. brown sugar, packed
1-1/2 c. butter, softened
3 eggs, beaten
2 t. almond extract
4-1/4 c. all-purpose flour

2 t. baking soda
1/2 t. salt
8-oz. pkg. semi-sweet
   chocolate chips
8-oz. pkg. white chocolate chips
1 c. fresh cranberries, halved

In a large bowl, beat sugars and butter until light and fluffy. Add eggs and extract; blend well. Add flour, baking soda and salt; mix well. Stir in chips and cranberries. Drop dough by rounded tablespoonfuls onto ungreased baking sheets, 2 inches apart. Bake at 375 degrees for 8 to 10 minutes, until lightly golden. Cool on wire racks. Makes 6 dozen.

Christmas bazaars are so much fun...jot the dates on your calendar and invite friends to come along. These get-togethers are filled with one-of-a-kind handmade items and scrumptious homebaked goodies that are just too good to pass up!

Festive
Sweets & Treats

Norwegian Tea Cakes

Jackie Flaherty
Saint Paul, MN

They pop in your mouth! The hour-long baking time is so worth it. I tried this recipe after using my "old" recipe for 30 years...there's no comparison.

1 c. butter, softened
1/4 c. sugar
1/2 t. salt
1 t. vanilla extract

2 c. cake flour
1 c. finely chopped pecans
Garnish: powdered sugar

In a large bowl, beat butter with an electric mixer on medium speed for 2 minutes, or until creamy. Add sugar and salt; beat for 3 minutes, or until light and fluffy. Beat in vanilla. Add flour; beat on low speed just until blended. Mix in pecans. Using floured hands, roll dough into one-inch balls, or use a small scoop. Place on ungreased baking sheets. Bake at 275 degrees for one hour. Remove from oven and let stand for 2 minutes. Roll warm cookies in powdered sugar; cool completely. Store in an airtight container. Makes 4 dozen.

A quick & easy sampler of goodies! Arrange ruffled paper candy cups in a holiday tin and fill each with a different treat. Try an assortment including fudge balls, sugar-coated nuts and bite-size cookies...yum!

Christmas
for Sharing

Easy Lemon Pound Cake

Judy Borecky
Escondido, CA

My mother made the most delicious pound cake. She was from Georgia and was over a hundred years old when she passed away. Here is my easy version. If you'd like to make a vanilla pound cake, use white cake mix with vanilla extract, and milk instead of lemon juice in the icing.

18-1/4 oz. pkg. lemon cake mix
1 c. sour cream
1 c. sugar
3 eggs, beaten

1/2 c. all-purpose flour
1/2 c. butter, softened
1 T. lemon extract
Optional: 1 T. poppy seed

Line the bottom of an angel food or tube cake pan with parchment paper strips. Spray with non-stick vegetable spray and set aside. In a large bowl, combine all ingredients except optional poppy seed. Beat with an electric mixer on medium-high speed until blended; stir in poppy seed, if using. Pour batter into cake pan. Bake at 350 degrees for one hour, or until a toothpick tests done. Turn out of pan; cool completely. Drizzle with Lemon Icing; slice and serve. Makes 10 to 12 servings.

Lemon Icing:

2 c. powdered sugar

3 T. lemon juice

Whisk together powdered sugar and lemon juice until blended.

Give your home a spicy holiday scent year 'round. Cover oranges with whole cloves, piercing the peels in swirly designs or simply covering the fruit at random. Roll in cinnamon and ginger, then stack in a wooden bowl. Once dried, the oranges will remain fragrant for months.

Festive
Sweets & Treats

Pistachio Meltaways

*Ann Davis
Brookville, IN*

*These cookies melt in your mouth! My family looks forward
to them every Christmas.*

1/2 c. powdered sugar
1/2 c. butter
1/2 c. shortening
2 eggs, beaten
1-1/2 t. almond extract
3-1/2 oz. box instant pistachio
    pudding mix

few drops green food coloring
2 c. all-purpose flour
1/2 t. baking soda
1/8 t. salt
1/4 c. sugar

In a large bowl, combine powdered sugar, butter, shortening, eggs, extract, dry pudding mix and food coloring; blend well. Add flour, baking soda and salt; mix well. Cover and refrigerate for at least one hour. Shape dough into one-inch balls; roll in sugar. Place balls on ungreased baking sheets, 2 inches apart. Bake at 375 degrees for 8 to 10 minutes. Cool cookies on wire racks. Makes one dozen.

Create a gingerbread house the easy way...no baking, just fun!
Find a house-shaped box, then turn everyone's imagination
loose with decorator frostings, assorted candies, even
cereal and pretzels. Be sure to have extra candies
on hand for nibbling!

Christmas
for Sharing

Santa's Crunch Cookies

Valerie Biggs-Montoya
North Edwards, CA

I make these every year with my kids at Christmastime. Then we watch "Santa Claus is Coming to Town" together while enjoying our cookies and peppermint hot chocolate. Throughout the rest of the year, this recipe can also double as a fantastic sugar cookie dough.

1 c. butter, softened
1-1/2 c. sugar
2 eggs, beaten
2 t. vanilla extract
2-3/4 c. all-purpose flour

1-1/2 t. baking powder
1/2 t. baking soda
1 t. salt
1 c. peppermint crunch
    baking chips

In a bowl, blend together butter, sugar, eggs and vanilla until well mixed; set aside. In another bowl, sift together flour, baking powder, baking soda and salt. Add flour mixture to butter mixture one cup at a time, beating with an electric mixer on low speed until well combined and a soft dough forms. Gently fold in peppermint chips. With a melon baller or a small cookie scoop, scoop dough onto parchment paper-lined baking sheets. Bake at 325 degrees for 20 minutes, or for 23 to 25 minutes if you prefer your cookies a little more golden. Remove to wire racks; cool. Makes 2 dozen.

Keep hot chocolate must-haves handy using vintage serving trays or enamelware cake pans. Marshmallows, whipped cream, shakers of cinnamon or cocoa and peppermint sticks will be right at your fingertips.

Festive
Sweets & Treats

Rudolph's Kisses

Julie Perkins
Anderson, IN

*These macaroon cookies are fun and easy to make with
the kids! They love putting the cherries in the center.
Don't forget to set some out some for Santa!*

14-oz. can sweetened
   condensed milk
14-oz. pkg. flaked coconut

2 t. vanilla extract
8-oz. container candied red
   cherries, divided

In a bowl, combine condensed milk, coconut, vanilla and 1/2 cup
chopped cherries; mix well. Drop dough by 1-1/2 tablespoonfuls onto
parchment paper-lined baking sheets. Cut remaining cherries in half;
press a cherry half onto each macaroon. Bake at 325 degrees for 10 to
12 minutes, until lightly golden. Cool for 5 minutes before removing
from baking sheet. Makes 3 dozen.

Snowballs

Vicki Van Donselaar
Cedar, IA

This is a great no-bake recipe that kids can help with.

1 c. butter, softened
1/2 c. crunchy peanut butter
3/4 c. powdered sugar
1/2 t. vanilla extract
2 c. rolled oats, uncooked

1 c. mini semi-sweet
   chocolate chips
Optional: 1 c. flaked coconut
Garnish: powdered sugar

In a large bowl, mix together all ingredients except garnish. Cover and
refrigerate for about one hour, until firm. Roll dough into balls by
tablespoonfuls; roll balls in powdered sugar. Keep refrigerated. Makes
3 to 4 dozen.

Small brown paper sacks chock-full
of homemade candies are thoughtful
giveaways to hand out as sweet
"glad-you-stopped-by" gifts.

Christmas
for Sharing

White Chocolate Cashew Carmelitas

Karen Wilson
Defiance, OH

I love cashews, so I decided to change my favorite carmelita recipe to use cashews and white chocolate chips. Yum!

14-oz. pkg. caramels, unwrapped
1/2 c. evaporated milk
2 c. old-fashioned oats, uncooked
1-3/4 c. all-purpose flour
1-1/2 c. brown sugar, packed
1 t. baking soda
1/2 t. salt
1 c. butter, melted
1-1/2 c. cashew halves
1 c. white chocolate chips

In a saucepan over medium-low heat, combine caramels and evaporated milk. Cook and stir until caramels are melted; set aside. In a bowl, mix oats, flour, brown sugar, baking soda and salt. Stir in melted butter until crumbly. Press half of dough into a greased 13"x9" baking pan. Bake at 350 degrees for 10 minutes. Remove from oven; sprinkle with cashews and chocolate chips. Spread caramel mixture over top. Sprinkle remaining dough over caramel layer and press down lightly. Bake an additional 10 to 15 minutes. Cool completely; cut into bars. Makes 2 dozen.

Dress up the mailbox with evergreen branches, berry bunches and a bow, secured with wire. Then tuck in a sweet surprise for the letter carrier...it's sure to be appreciated!

Festive
Sweets & Treats

Grandma's Peppermint Brownies

*Kimberly Lottman
Big Island, VA*

This recipe is so simple, but so good! My paternal grandmother made these brownies every year for Christmas. One bite transports me right back to her kitchen on Christmas morning.

1-1/2 c. all-purpose flour
1-3/4 to 2 c. sugar
1/2 c. baking cocoa
1 c. oil or applesauce
4 eggs, beaten
1/4 c. water

1 t. salt
1 t. peppermint extract
1 t. vanilla extract
Garnish: chocolate frosting,
    crushed candy canes

In a large bowl, combine all ingredients except garnish; mix well. Pour batter into a greased 13"x9" baking pan. Bake at 350 degrees for 30 minutes, or until set. Cool completely. Spread with frosting; sprinkle with crushed candy canes. Cut into bars. Makes 12 to 15.

Make clean-up a snap for brownies and bar cookies. Before pouring the batter into the baking pan, line it with aluminum foil, leaving extra foil on both ends for "handles." Once the brownies have cooled completely, lift them out by the foil handles. Peel off the foil and cut into bars.

Christmas
for Sharing

Holiday Cookies

*Linda Diepholz
Lakeville, MN*

These cookies are easy and delicious I like to use candy-coated chocolates in seasonal colors to dress them up for all the various holidays.

16-1/4 oz. pkg. yellow cake
  mix, divided
1/2 c. butter, softened
3 T. dark brown sugar, packed
2 eggs, beaten

2 t. vanilla extract
11-oz. pkg. candy-coated
  chocolates
Optional: 1 c. chopped pecans
  or walnuts

In a large bowl, combine half of the dry cake mix, butter, brown sugar, eggs and vanilla. Beat with an electric mixer on medium-high speed for one to 2 minutes. Add remaining cake mix. Beat for one minute, or until all ingredients are moistened. Fold in candies and nuts, if using. Drop dough by teaspoonfuls onto baking sheets coated with non-stick vegetable spray, 2 inches apart, Bake at 350 degrees for 10 to 13 minutes, until cookies are golden at the edges and centers are just barely set. Cool cookies on baking sheets for one minute. Transfer to wire racks and cool completely. Makes 3 dozen.

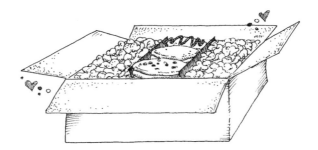

Follow these tips for mailing a gift of cookies. Choose firm cookies like sliced, drop or bar cookies; avoid frosted or filled ones. Line a sturdy box with plastic bubble wrap and pack cookies in single layers, with wax paper between the layers. Your cookies will arrive fresh, unbroken and full of love!

Festive
Sweets & Treats

Desperation Dandies

Elizabeth Smithson
Mayfield, KY

Also known as Christmas Critters! I found this recipe years ago in a farm magazine, and it became a Christmas favorite for our cookie exchange. Try different kinds of nuts...they're all good!

14-oz. can sweetened
   condensed milk
3 6-oz. pkgs. semi-sweet
   chocolate chips

1/2 c. butter
2 c. mini marshmallows
2 c. chopped pecans or walnuts

In a saucepan over medium heat, combine condensed milk, chocolate chips and butter. Cook and stir until chocolate chips melt. Remove from heat; stir until well mixed. Add marshmallows and nuts; mix well. Drop mixture by teaspoonfuls onto wax paper-covered baking sheets; chill for 2 hours. Cover and store at room temperature or refrigerate. Makes 2 dozen.

Variation: To save time, spread chocolate mixture in a buttered 13"x9" baking pan; chill and cut into small squares.

Dress up cookies in a jiffy! Melt semi-sweet or white chocolate, then dip half of each cookie into chocolate. Quickly sprinkle with colorful sprinkles or chopped peppermints...done!

Christmas
for Sharing

Red Velvet Layer Cake

Sherry Page
Akron, OH

This recipe reminds me of the cake my grandma used to make for us. This is the closest to hers that I could find.

1/2 c. butter, softened	1 c. buttermilk
1-1/2 c. sugar	1 t. salt
3 eggs, beaten	1 t. vanilla extract
2 T. baking cocoa	1-1/2 t. baking soda
1-oz. bottle red food coloring	1 T. vinegar
2-1/4 c. all-purpose flour	

In a large bowl, blend together butter, sugar and eggs; set aside. In a small bowl, make a paste of cocoa and food coloring; add to butter mixture and mix well. Add flour, buttermilk, salt and vanilla; mix well. Fold in baking soda and vinegar. Pour batter into 2 greased and floured 8" round cake pans. Bake at 350 degrees for about 30 minutes, until a toothpick inserted in the center comes out clean. Cool; assemble layers with Icing and frost the outside of cake. Makes 12 to 15 servings.

Icing:

1 c. milk	1 c. sugar
5 T. all-purpose flour	1 t. vanilla extract
1 c. butter, softened	

In the top of a double boiler, cook and stir milk and flour until thickened; cool. In a bowl, blend butter, sugar and vanilla; beat well. Add butter mixture to cooled flour mixture; beat to a spreadable consistency.

When frosting a layer cake, tuck strips of wax paper under the edges of the bottom layer. Remove them after the cake is frosted, for a neat and tidy cake plate with no frosting smudges.

Festive
Sweets & Treats

Cheesecake Puff Pie

Kisha Landeros
Pacific, MO

This is one of the first dessert recipes I learned how to make in my grandma's kitchen. It is super-easy, always a hit and brings back memories of all of our family get-togethers. We love it because it is so simple and looks very pretty when displayed on a platter...and because it is delicious, of course!

8-oz. tube refrigerated crescent
  rolls, divided
2 8-oz. pkgs. cream cheese,
  softened

2 c. sugar
1 T. vanilla extract
21-oz. can cherry pie filling or
  other fruit pie filling

Cover the bottom of a 9" pie plate with several crescent rolls, stretching them to fit while leaving some overhang; set aside. In a bowl, blend together cream cheese, sugar and vanilla; spoon over crescents in pie plate. Arrange remaining crescent rolls on top, pressing the edges together to fully cover. Bake at 350 degrees for 20 to 25 minutes, until crescents are golden. Let cool; turn out onto a serving platter. Spoon pie filling over pie. Cover and chill until serving time. Cut into wedges; serve chilled. Makes 8 servings.

Oh, heart, let's never grow too old
To smile anew, when Christmas comes,
At tassels red and tinsel thread,
And tarlatan bags of sugarplums.

–Nancy Byrd Turner

Christmas
for Sharing

Crème de Menthe Brownies

Bessie Branyon
Birmingham, AL

This recipe was given to me by a former Minister of Music at our church. The family has moved out of state, but when we are together, it seems as if time and distance don't matter.

1 c. sugar	4 eggs, beaten
1 c. all- purpose flour, sifted	16-oz. can chocolate syrup
1/2 t. salt	1 T. vanilla extract
1/2 c. margarine, softened	1/2 c. chopped nuts

Combine sugar, flour and salt in a large bowl; stir well. Stir in margarine, eggs, chocolate syrup and vanilla. Fold in nuts; pour batter into a greased and floured 14"x10" baking pan. Bake at 325 degrees for 30 minutes; cool completely. Spread Filling over cooled brownies; spread cooled Icing over filling. Refrigerate for 4 hours; cut into squares and serve. Makes 1-1/2 to 2 dozen.

Filling:

1/2 c. margarine, softened	2 T. crème de menthe
2 c. powdered sugar, sifted	

Beat margarine until smooth. Add powdered sugar; beat until smooth. Stir in crème de menthe.

Icing:

6-oz. pkg. semi-sweet chocolate chips	6 T. margarine

Melt chocolate chips with margarine in a saucepan over medium-low heat; cool. Stir until smooth; cool.

Festive
Sweets & Treats

Candy Hash

Nancy Kaiser
York, SC

At Christmastime, I make several cookie & candy trays. This is one of the treats that I include...it always get rave reviews. I usually make a double batch, so I have plenty to go around. It's very quick & easy to make.

1 lb. white candy melts
1/4 c. creamy peanut butter

1-1/4 c. salted peanuts
2-1/2 c. pretzels, broken up

Combine candy melts and peanut butter in a microwave-safe bowl. Microwave on high at 15-second intervals until melted; stir. Add peanuts and pretzels; stir until thoroughly coated. Scoop mixture with a small candy scoop onto a wax paper-lined baking sheet. Let stand until set; may refrigerate for 10 minutes to set faster. Store in an airtight container at room temperature. Makes 3 to 4 dozen.

Dad's Butterscotch Candy

Joan Chance
Houston, TX

My dad could cook two things...milk toast (yuck!) when Mom wasn't well, and this candy...yum! This delicious candy became his specialty.

1-1/2 c. sugar
3/4 c. water
6 T. light corn syrup

3 T. butter, sliced
1 t. vanilla extract

In a heavy saucepan over medium heat, combine sugar, water and corn syrup. Bring to a boil; cook without stirring for 5 minutes. Add butter; cook until mixture reaches the hard-crack stage, or 300 to 310 degrees on a candy thermometer. Remove from heat; stir in vanilla. Pour mixture into a buttered baking sheet, or drop onto a buttered piece of parchment paper for individual candies. Cool and let harden. Crack candy into pieces. Serves 10 to 12.

Christmas
for Sharing

Grandma's Sugar Cookies

Lisa Hoch
Salem, OH

This is my grandma's cookie recipe that has been in the family since I was a little girl. It is still the most-requested recipe in our family for Christmas cookies. They are so moist and delicious! The dough can be rolled for cut-outs, or made as drop cookies.

2 eggs, beaten
2 c. sugar
1 c. shortening
1 t. vanilla extract
1 c. milk

5 c. all-purpose flour
4 t. baking powder
1 t. baking soda
1/8 t. salt
Optional: candy sprinkles

In a large bowl, mix eggs, sugar, shortening and vanilla until creamy. Slowly mix in milk; set aside. In a small bowl, combine remaining ingredients except optional sprinkles; gradually stir flour mixture into egg mixture. Roll out dough 1/4-inch thick on a floured surface; cut with cookie cutters and place on greased baking sheets. Bake at 350 degrees for 6 to 8 minutes, until golden. Cool cookies on wire racks. Spread with Icing; if desired, decorate with sprinkles before icing hardens. Makes 3 to 4 dozen.

Drop Cookies: use only 4-1/4 cups flour; drop by teaspoonfuls onto lightly greased baking sheets. Bake at 350 degrees for 8 to 10 minutes, until golden.

Icing:

1/2 c. shortening
1/2 c. butter, softened
1/2 t. vanilla extract

4 c. powdered sugar
1 to 2 T. milk
Optional: food coloring

Stir together shortening, butter and vanilla until creamy. Slowly stir in powdered sugar and milk, one tablespoon of milk at a time, to desired consistency. Add a few drops food coloring, if desired.

Festive
Sweets & Treats

Fanciful Raspberry Ribbons

Sylvia Stachura
Mesa, AZ

Every Christmas baking season in our household starts with this recipe. These cookies are always the first to be chosen from the holiday cookie platter that's passed around!

1 c. butter, softened
2-1/2 c. all-purpose flour, divided
1/2 c. sugar

1 egg, lightly beaten
1 t. vanilla extract
1/4 t. salt
Garnish: raspberry jam

In a large bowl, beat butter with an electric mixer on medium speed until fluffy. Add half of flour, sugar, egg, vanilla and salt; beat until thoroughly combined. Beat in remaining flour, mixing until dough sticks together to form a ball. Gather dough into a ball and knead slightly. Divide dough into 8 equal portions. On a lightly floured surface, roll out each portion into a 9-inch-long rope. Arrange dough ropes on ungreased baking sheets, about 2 inches apart. With a wooden spoon handle, press a long groove down the length of each rope. Bake at 375 degrees for 10 minutes. Remove from oven; spoon jam into grooves. Bake for another 5 minutes, or until edges are lightly golden. Cool on baking sheets for 5 minutes. Using a large spatula, remove baked ropes to a cutting board. While still warm, drizzle with Powdered Sugar Glaze; cut diagonally into one-inch slices. Makes 6 dozen.

Powdered Sugar Glaze:

3/4 c. powdered sugar
1/4 t. almond extract

3 to 4 t. milk

In a bowl, mix all ingredients until smooth, adding enough milk for a drizzling consistency.

A joy that's shared is
a joy made double.
–John Ray

Christmas
for Sharing

No-Fail Happy Holidays Fudge

Debra Arch
Kewanee, IL

This rich chocolatey fudge is made with simple ingredients and always turns out smooth and creamy. The recipe makes plenty for sharing, too.

2 T. butter
2/3 c. evaporated milk
1-2/3 c. sugar
1/2 t. salt
1 t. vanilla extract

2 c. mini marshmallows
1-1/2 c. semi-sweet chocolate
  chips
Optional: 1/2 c. chopped nuts

In a heavy saucepan over medium heat, melt butter with milk, sugar and salt; bring to a boil. Boil for 4 minutes, stirring constantly. Remove from heat; add remaining ingredients. Stir vigorously for one minute, or until marshmallows are melted and blended. Pour fudge into a buttered 8"x8" baking pan; cool completely and cut into squares. Makes about 5-1/2 dozen pieces.

Watch yard sales for like-new Christmas tins, canning jars and other containers to fill with holiday goodies for gift giving. Dress up jar lids with a pinked circle of calico, or glue on buttons and charms...tins just need a liner of parchment paper. Clever!

Festive
Sweets & Treats

Easy Creamy Peanut Butter Fudge

Karen Sampson
Waymart, PA

This is the easiest fudge I have ever made! I like to make several batches to sell at the holiday bake sale at our church and to give away as gifts. It is so creamy, everyone loves it!

2 c. sugar
1/2 c. milk

1-1/3 c. creamy peanut butter
7-oz. jar marshmallow creme

In a heavy saucepan over medium heat, bring sugar and milk to a boil. Boil for 3 minutes. Add peanut butter and marshmallow creme; mix until well blended. Quickly pour fudge into a buttered 8"x8" baking pan; cover and chill until set. Cut into squares. Makes 3 to 4 dozen pieces.

Butterscotch Nibbles

Vicki Van Donselaar
Cedar, IA

Every year, my husband's side of the family makes this crunchy, yummy treat as part of our candy-making day.

8 c. bite-size crispy corn
  cereal squares
12-oz. pkg. butterscotch chips

1 c. creamy peanut butter
1 c. semi-sweet chocolate chips

Add cereal to a large heat-proof bowl; set aside. In a heavy saucepan over medium heat, combine butterscotch chips and peanut butter; cook and stir until melted. Pour over cereal; stir until coated. Add chocolate chips; stir until combined and mixture looks marbled. Spread mixture in a buttered 17"x11" jelly-roll pan. Cool for 30 minutes; break up and store in an airtight container. Makes 2 to 2-1/2 dozen pieces.

If a nest in your Christmas
tree is to be found,
Love and good fortune will be
yours the year 'round.

–Old tradition

Christmas
for Sharing

Almond-Orange Loaf Cake

Aqsa Masood
Ontario, Canada

I came up with this recipe one really cold, chilly day when my daughter requested orange cake. She just loves oranges and almonds! Believe me, it is a perfect comfort dessert on such cold winter evenings to share with your loved ones. Enjoy with a hot cup of coffee.

1 c. all-purpose flour
1/2 c. almond flour
1 c. sugar
1 T. unsweetened flaked coconut
1 t. baking powder
1/4 t. baking soda
1/8 t. salt
Optional: 1 t. cinnamon

1 c. orange juice
1/2 c. butter, melted
1/4 c. oil
2 eggs, beaten
1 t. vanilla extract
Optional: 2 T. apricot jam,
    2 to 3 T. hot water

In a large bowl, combine flours, sugar, coconut, baking powder, baking soda, salt and cinnamon, if using. Mix well and set aside. In another bowl, combine orange juice, butter, oil, eggs and vanilla. Beat with an electric mixer on medium speed until well combined. Add juice mixture to flour mixture. Beat on medium to high speed for 2 to 3 minutes, until a ribbon effect forms in the batter. Pour batter into a greased or parchment paper-lined 9"x5" heavy-bottomed loaf pan. Bake at 375 degrees for 40 minutes, or until a toothpick inserted in center comes out clean. Cool cake completely; turn out of pan. If desired, combine apricot jam and enough hot water for a glaze consistency; spread over cake. Let stand for 30 minutes after glazing; slice and serve. Makes 6 to 8 servings.

Bake your favorite fruit bread in mini loaves for welcome gifts.
Wrap individually in colored cellophane or colorful tea towels,
or just tie a ribbon around the loaf pan!

Festive
Sweets & Treats

Triple Chocolate Pecan Pie

Donna Wilson
Maryville, TN

This is a recipe that my kids loved every year they were growing up. Now that they're older, they are making it for their own children as well. A favorite for the whole holiday season!

1 c. white chocolate chips
1 c. dark chocolate chips
1/2 c. milk chocolate chips
9-inch pie crust, unbaked
1 c. chopped pecans
2 eggs, beaten

2/3 c. brown sugar, packed
1/2 c. dark corn syrup
2 T. butter, melted
1 t. vanilla extract
1/2 t. salt

Add all chocolate chips to pie crust; mix gently. Top with pecans and set aside. Combine remaining ingredients in a bowl. Mix well; spoon mixture over chips and pecans in crust. Bake at 425 degrees for 15 minutes. Reduce oven temperature to 350 degrees. Continue baking for 30 minutes longer, or until lightly golden on top. Cool completely; cut into wedges. Makes 6 to 8 servings.

If your baked dessert didn't turn out quite right, layer it with whipped cream in a parfait glass and give it a fancy name. It will still be scrumptious...and nobody will know the difference!

Christmas
for Sharing

Gingersnap Cookies

Sue Troth
Alberta, Canada

These are the best gingersnaps my family has ever tasted! The recipe was shared by a customer at my travel agency. She was a cook on oil rigs in North Alberta. They are terrific...freeze very well, too.

3 c. all-purpose flour
2 t. baking soda
1 t. salt
1 t. cinnamon
1 t. ground ginger
1/2 t. ground cloves

3/4 c. shortening
3/4 c. brown sugar, packed
3/4 c. dark molasses
1 egg, beaten
1/2 c. sugar

In a large bowl, sift together flour, baking soda, salt and spices; set aside. In another bowl, blend together shortening, brown sugar, molasses and egg. Cover and chill overnight. Roll dough into balls, 2 tablespoons per ball; dip in sugar. Arrange on ungreased baking sheets; flatten with the bottom of a glass tumbler. Bake at 350 degrees for 8 to 9 minutes, watching carefully to avoid burning. Makes 3 dozen.

Toffee Chocolate Squares

Michelle Newlin
Portage, PA

These sweet treats can be customized with color-themed candies and sprinkles to match any holiday or occasion!

1 sleeve saltine crackers
1 c. butter
1 c. brown sugar, packed
1-3/4 c. semi-sweet
  chocolate chips

Garnish: candy-coated chocolates
and/or candy sprinkles

Line a rimmed 15"x10" jelly-roll pan with aluminum foil; coat with non-stick vegetable spray. Line pan with crackers; set aside. In a saucepan over medium heat, melt butter with brown sugar. Bring to a boil, stirring continuously; cook for about 2 minutes, until bubbling. Spoon evenly over crackers. Bake at 350 degrees for 12 to 15 minutes. Remove from oven; immediately top with chocolate chips. Let stand until melted; smooth chocolate out into an even layer. Garnish as desired. Cut into squares; let cool until set. Makes 3 dozen.

Festive
Sweets & Treats

Fruitcake Cookies

Tina Matie
Alma, GA

I remember going to my grandparents' home around the holidays. My grandmother always had these fruitcake cookies ready for us. When you walked in the door, the wonderful smell of the cookies lingered all over her house. They were so delicious...still are! Now, whenever I make these cookies, it always brings back memories of going to my grandparents' home around the holidays. These are still a family favorite.

8-oz. container candied green
    cherries, chopped
8-oz. container red cherries,
    chopped
8-oz. container candied
    pineapple, chopped

1 c. self-rising flour
5 c. chopped pecans
14-oz. can sweetened
    condensed milk
3/4 c. butter, melted

Combine fruits in a large bowl, sprinkle with flour and toss to coat. Add nuts, condensed milk and melted butter; mix together well. Spoon mixture into greased mini muffin cups. Bake at 350 degrees for 20 minutes. Cool on wire racks. Makes 6 dozen.

Kitchen scissors are a handy helper. Grab 'em to make quick work of cutting up sticky candied fruits...cut right into the mixing bowl!

Christmas
for Sharing

Lee's Ambrosia Deluxe

Leona Krivda
Belle Vernon, PA

This is a recipe that my grandson Jensen often requested for me to bring to their house for Christmas day. It is always a big hit!

2 c. fresh cranberries, halved
1/2 c. sugar
20-oz. can pineapple tidbits,
   very well drained
15-oz. can mandarin oranges,
   very well drained and halved
2 c. apples, cored and diced

1 c. seedless red grapes, halved
3/4 c. chopped pecans
3 c. mini marshmallows
2 c. whipping cream
12-oz. container frozen whipped
   topping, thawed and divided
1 to 2 c. shredded coconut

In a bowl, mix together cranberries and sugar; set aside for about 20 minutes. In a large bowl, combine remaining fruits, pecans and marshmallows; mix gently. Fold in cranberry mixture; set aside. In another bowl, beat cream with an electric mixer on high speed until stiff peaks form; fold in most of whipped topping. Fold whipped cream mixture into fruit mixture. Add desired amount of coconut; fold in well. Cover and chill till serving time. If mixture seems a little dry, add a little more whipped topping. Serves 8.

Be sure to share family tales at Christmastime...they're super conversation starters. How about the time Grandma set out cookies to cool and her dog Skippy ate them, or the year a big snowstorm led to a houseful of extra Christmas guests... it's such fun to share stories like these!

Festive
Sweets & Treats

Pistachio Holiday Ice Cream Dessert

Edward Kielar
Whitehouse, OH

The green color and toffee topping make this a holiday-ready dessert.

1 c. buttery round crackers, crushed
1/4 c. butter, melted
3/4 c. cold milk
3.4-oz. pkg. instant pistachio pudding mix

1 qt. vanilla ice cream, softened
8-oz. container frozen whipped topping, thawed
2 1.4-oz. chocolate-covered toffee candy bars, crushed

Combine cracker crumbs and butter in a bowl; mix well. Press into an ungreased 9"x9" baking pan. Bake at 325 degrees for 7 to 10 minutes, until lightly golden. Cool in pan on a wire rack. Meanwhile, in a large bowl, whisk milk and dry pudding mix for 2 minutes. Let stand for 2 minutes, or until softly set. Fold in ice cream; spoon over baked crust. Cover and freeze for 2 hours, or until firm. Spread with whipped topping; sprinkle with crushed candy bars. Cover and freeze for one hour, or until firm. To serve, let stand at room temperature several minutes; cut into squares. Serves 8.

A special touch for holiday desserts! Be sure to pick up
a pint or 2 of ice cream in peppermint, cinnamon
and other seasonal flavors.

Christmas
for Sharing

Cornmeal Crunchies

Carol Brownridge
Ontario, Canada

These cut-out cookies are great for Christmas cookie exchanges. I even make them year 'round, whenever I feel like something crunchy and sweet. You can tailor them to any holiday or special occasion by using different cookie-cutter shapes and candy sprinkles.

3/4 c. butter, softened
3/4 c. sugar
1 egg, beaten
1 t. vanilla extract
1-1/2 c. all-purpose flour
1/2 c. cornmeal

1 t. baking powder
1/4 t. salt
Optional: 1/2 c. raisins
1 c. semi-sweet chocolate chips
Garnish: candy sprinkles

In a large bowl, beat butter with sugar. Add egg and vanilla; beat well and set aside. In a separate bowl, mix flour, cornmeal, baking powder and salt. Add to butter mixture and stir well. Stir in raisins, if using. Form dough into a ball; wrap in plastic wrap and chill for one hour. Roll dough out to 1/4-inch thickness on a floured surface. Cut with cookie cutters; arrange on lightly greased baking sheets, one inch apart. Bake at 350 degrees for 10 to 12 minutes; cool on wire racks. Add chocolate chips to a microwave-safe bowl. Microwave on high for 2 minutes, stirring occasionally, or until melted and smooth. Dip cookies into melted chocolate; add sprinkles on top and let stand until chocolate sets. Makes 3 dozen.

If you need just a little colored sugar for cookies, make it yourself. Just place 1/4 cup sugar in a small jar, add a drop or 2 of food coloring, cover the jar and shake to blend well. Spread the sugar on wax paper and let dry.

Festive
Sweets & Treats

Festive Cranberry Upside-Down Cake

Lisa Ann Panzino DiNunzio
Vineland, NJ

Beautiful, sweet, tart and delicious...easy to make, too!

18-1/4 oz. pkg. yellow cake mix
1/2 c. butter
1 c. brown sugar, packed

12-oz. pkg. fresh or frozen
cranberries

In a large bowl, prepare cake mix as directed on package; set aside batter. In a 13"x9" baking pan, melt butter in oven at 350 degrees. Sprinkle brown sugar evenly over butter; sprinkle cranberries over brown sugar. Pour cake batter over cranberries. Bake at 350 degrees for 28 to 33 minutes, until a toothpick inserted in center tests clean. Immediately run a knife around side of pan to loosen cake. Let cake cool for one minute. Place a serving plate upside-down onto cake pan; turn plate and pan over. Leave pan over cake for one minute, to allow brown sugar topping to drizzle over cake. Give a gentle tap and remove pan; cool for 30 minutes. Cut into squares. Makes 12 servings.

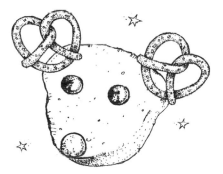

Reindeer cookies are fun for kids. Shape sugar cookie dough into one-inch balls. Pinch one side of the ball to form a point and gently flatten it. Bake as directed; remove from oven. Immediately press in 2 mini pretzels for antlers, 2 mini brown candy-coated chocolates for eyes and a regular-size red candy-coated chocolate nose.

Christmas
for Sharing

Old-Fashioned Rice Pudding

Shannon Reents
Poland, OH

This was my Great-Aunt Grace's recipe. I can remember going to her country farm when I was about 12 and knowing she would have this scrumptious rice pudding waiting when I got there. Not just for me... but she knew it was my favorite!

1/2 c. long-cooking rice,
   uncooked
4 c. milk
1/3 c. sugar

1/2 t. salt
1/2 t. cinnamon
Optional: 1/2 c. raisins

Cook rice according to package directions. Transfer to a lightly greased 1-1/2 quart casserole dish; set aside. Heat milk in a saucepan over medium heat; stir in sugar, salt and cinnamon. Bring to a boil; add to rice in dish. Bake, uncovered, at 325 degrees for 1-1/2 hours, or until almost set, stirring every 20 minutes. If desired, stir in raisins about 20 minutes before pudding is done. Serves 6 to 8.

Grandma Emma's Raisin Pudding

Leona Krivda
Belle Vernon, PA

Even though my Grandma Emma passed before I was born, I am so thankful that some of her recipes were passed down. This is one that I made for my dad, who was her son, quite often. He always talked about her when we enjoyed it with a cup of coffee.

3-1/3 c. boiling water
3-1/2 c. light brown sugar,
   packed and divided
3 T. shortening
3 c. all-purpose flour
2 T. baking powder

3/4 t. salt
1-1/2 c. milk
1 T. vanilla extract
1-1/2 c. raisins
1-1/2 c. chopped walnuts

Grease the bottom of a 13"x9" baking pan. Add boiling water and 2 cups brown sugar to pan; stir a little to cover bottom of pan evenly. Set aside. In a large bowl, blend shortening and remaining brown sugar. Add flour, baking powder and salt alternately with milk; mix well. Stir in vanilla. Fold in raisins and walnuts; pour batter into pan. Bake, uncovered, at 350 degrees for 35 to 40 minutes. Serves 10 to 12.

Festive
Sweets & Treats

Grandma Great's Banana Bread Pudding

Sandy Coffey
Cincinnati, OH

This is Great-Grandma's yummy dessert that the whole family loves. Great for any holiday or Sunday dinner...and it makes plenty for everybody!

16 eggs
2 qts. whipping cream
2 c. sugar

1/2 c. vanilla extract
8 c. day-old bread, cut into cubes
3 c. very ripe bananas, sliced

In a large bowl, beat eggs well. Add cream, sugar and vanilla; beat well and set aside. Place bread cubes in a lightly greased 13"x9" baking pan. Arrange banana slices over bread; spoon egg mixture over all. Let stand at room temperature for 3 minutes. Cover and bake at 350 degrees for 40 minutes. Uncover; bake for a few more minutes, until lightly golden. Serve warm or at room temperature. Serves 12 to 16.

Share the Christmas spirit with a good deed...shovel a neighbor's sidewalk and driveway. When you reach the doorstep, be sure to knock on the door and wish them a happy holiday. You might want to take them a plate of cookies, too!

Christmas
for Sharing

Grandma Laub's Cherry-Coconut Bars

Jan Keith
Jackson, MO

My grandma and her sister would start baking at least a month before Christmas. They stored all kinds of cookies in old-fashioned 5-gallon lard tins. Everyone got a box of assorted treats! This one was my favorite. The recipe may be doubled, using a 13x9 pan for the pastry.

2 eggs, lightly beaten
1 c. sugar
1/4 c. all-purpose flour
1/2 t. baking powder
1/4 t. salt
1 t. vanilla extract

3/4 c. chopped pecans
1/2 c. flaked coconut
1/2 c. maraschino cherries,
   drained and quartered
Garnish: powdered sugar

Make Pastry and bake; set aside to cool. For filling, combine all ingredients except garnish in a large bowl. Mix well; spread over baked pastry. Bake at 350 degrees for 25 minutes. Cool; cut into bars. Dust with additional powdered sugar. Makes one dozen.

Pastry:

1 c. all-purpose flour, sifted
1/2 c. butter

3 T. powdered sugar

Mix flour, butter and powdered sugar until smooth. Spread in a lightly greased 8"x8" baking pan. Bake at 350 degrees for 25 minutes, or until lightly golden; let cool.

When you go out on Christmas Eve to attend church or see the Christmas lights, why not drop off a dozen fresh-baked cookies at a local police or fire station?

Festive
Sweets & Treats

Cranberry-Apple Crisp

Sue Klapper
Muskego, WI

This is a great comfort dessert when it's cold and snowy here in Wisconsin! It's very simple to make.

5 Granny Smith apples, peeled, cored, sliced and cut crosswise
15-oz. can whole-berry cranberry sauce
1/4 c. sugar
1/3 c. plus 2 T. all-purpose flour, divided

1/4 c. chopped nuts
1 c. rolled oats, uncooked
1/3 c. brown sugar, packed
1 t. cinnamon
1/4 c. butter, melted
Optional: vanilla ice cream or whipped topping

Arrange apples in a lightly greased 3-quart deep casserole dish; set aside. In a bowl, combine cranberry sauce, sugar and 2 tablespoons flour; mix well and spoon over apples. Toss to coat evenly; set aside. For topping, combine remaining flour, chopped nuts, oats, brown sugar and cinnamon. Add melted butter; mix well. Sprinkle topping over fruit mixture. Bake at 375 degrees for 35 to 40 minutes, until fruit is tender. Serve warm, topped with ice cream or whipped topping if desired. Makes 10 servings.

After a big snowfall, whip up some good old-fashioned snow ice cream with the kids. Beat one cup whipping cream until soft peaks form, then fold in 4 cups freshly fallen snow. Add sugar and vanilla to taste. A wonderful wintertime treat!

Christmas
for Sharing

Creamy Caramel Frosting

Pat Beach
Fisherville, KY

*Our family has been enjoying this mouthwatering frosting recipe
for well over 60 years! It is so delicious on all kinds of cakes. My
husband's mother always used this recipe to frost a yellow cake. It's
also fabulous on spice, chocolate or even blackberry cake. We even
love it spread over homemade or store-bought apple pies.*

1/2 c. butter
1 c. brown sugar, packed
1/4 t. salt
1/4 c. milk

2-1/2 c. powdered sugar, sifted
1/2 t. vanilla extract
Optional: small amount
    whipping cream

Melt butter in a large saucepan over low heat; stir in brown sugar and
salt. Cook for 2 minutes, stirring constantly. Add milk; continue cooking
and stirring until mixture comes to a rolling boil. Remove from heat.
Gradually stir in powdered sugar. Add vanilla and mix well. Thin with a
small amount of cream, if frosting is too thick to spread. Makes enough
to frost a 13"x9" cake. For a 2-layer cake, use 1-1/2 to 2 times this
recipe.

Turn a Bundt® cake into a holiday wreath. Drizzle with frosting
and sprinkle with chopped candied cherries. Twist a strip of
red fruit leather into a jaunty bow to complete the wreath.

Festive
Sweets & Treats

Easy Chocolate Glaze

Suzanne Stroud
Bremen, GA

This is the icing my mom always used on our chocolate birthday cakes, growing up. Now it's the only "icing" my husband likes. It's so much better than store-bought, yet so easy. We generally serve this drizzled over Bundt® cakes, but it would be great on brownies or chocolate doughnuts...or just straight out of the bowl!

1/2 c. semi-sweet chocolate chips   2 T. milk
1 T. butter   1/2 c. powdered sugar, sifted

Combine chocolate chips, butter and milk in a microwave-safe bowl. Microwave on high for one minute; stir until chips are melted and smooth. If needed, microwave again for 15 to 20 seconds, watching closely. Gradually stir in powdered sugar until smooth and shiny. Spoon or drizzle over cake. If too thin, add a touch more powdered sugar; if too thick, add a little milk. Makes enough to glaze one Bundt® cake.

Aunt Nellie's Sweet Whipped Cream

Julie Perkins
Anderson, IN

Luscious on homemade desserts of all kinds.

1 c. whipping cream   1/2 t. vanilla extract
2 to 3 T. powdered sugar   1/8 t. salt

In a bowl, beat cream with an electric mixer on high speed until stiff peaks form. Mix in powdered sugar, vanilla and salt; continue to beat until well blended. Use immediately. Makes about 2 cups.

Brighten a party coffee tray...
stir a teaspoon of sparkly red
decorator sugar into the
sugar bowl!

INDEX

INDEX

INDEX

Find Gooseberry Patch
wherever you are!

www.gooseberrypatch.com

Call us toll-free at 1·800·854·6673

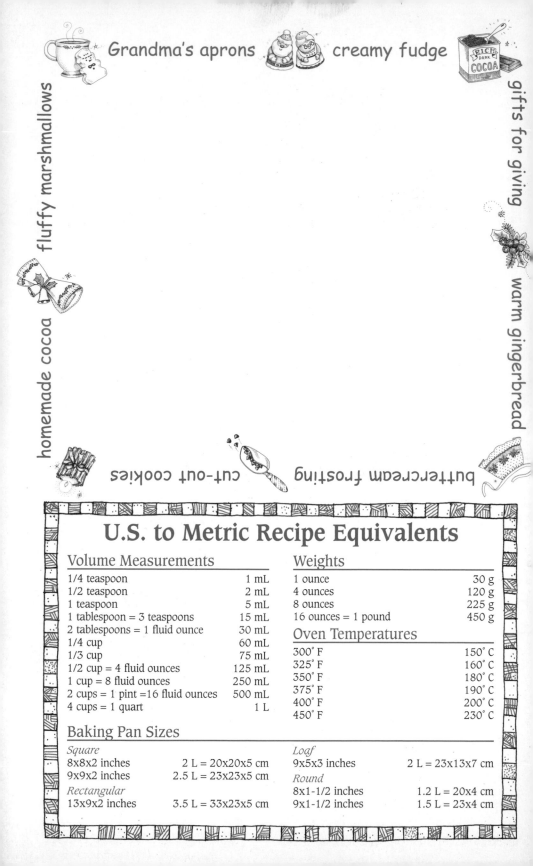

Grandma's aprons   creamy fudge

fluffy marshmallows

gifts for giving

homemade cocoa

warm gingerbread

cut-out cookies   buttercream frosting

U.S. to Metric Recipe Equivalents

Volume Measurements

1/4 teaspoon	1 mL
1/2 teaspoon	2 mL
1 teaspoon	5 mL
1 tablespoon = 3 teaspoons	15 mL
2 tablespoons = 1 fluid ounce	30 mL
1/4 cup	60 mL
1/3 cup	75 mL
1/2 cup = 4 fluid ounces	125 mL
1 cup = 8 fluid ounces	250 mL
2 cups = 1 pint =16 fluid ounces	500 mL
4 cups = 1 quart	1 L

Weights

1 ounce	30 g
4 ounces	120 g
8 ounces	225 g
16 ounces = 1 pound	450 g

Oven Temperatures

300° F	150° C
325° F	160° C
350° F	180° C
375° F	190° C
400° F	200° C
450° F	230° C

Baking Pan Sizes

Square		*Loaf*	
8x8x2 inches	2 L = 20x20x5 cm	9x5x3 inches	2 L = 23x13x7 cm
9x9x2 inches	2.5 L = 23x23x5 cm	*Round*	
Rectangular		8x1-1/2 inches	1.2 L = 20x4 cm
13x9x2 inches	3.5 L = 33x23x5 cm	9x1-1/2 inches	1.5 L = 23x4 cm